VIN SCULLY

THE VOICE OF DODGER BASEBALL

1927-2022

State Farm

Spectrum

Security Benefit | VIN | VINCENT EDWARD SCULLY 1927-2022 | Security Benefit

VINCENT EDWARD SCULLY 1927-2022

cpk

Security Benefit

YAAMAVA' RESORT & CASINO AT SAN MANUEL

UCLA Health

MORTON

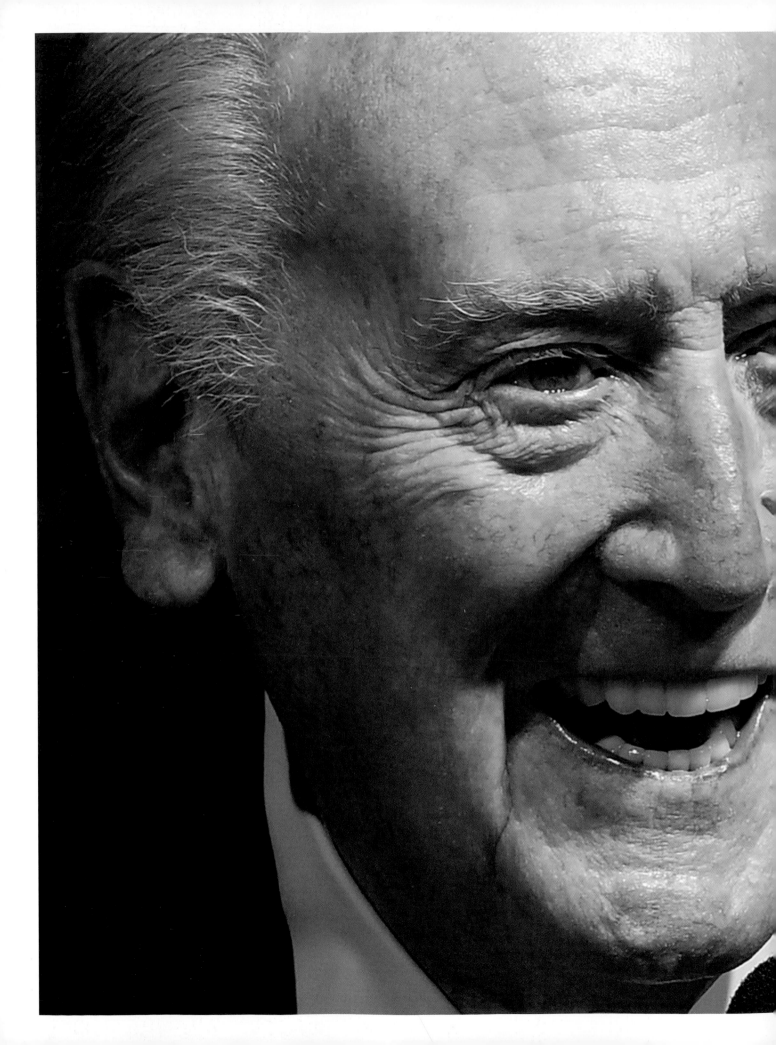

This book is available in quantity at special discounts for your group or organization.
For further information, contact:

Triumph Books LLC
814 North Franklin Street
Chicago, Illinois 60610
Phone: (312) 337-0747
www.triumphbooks.com

Printed in U.S.A.
ISBN: 978-1- 63727-308-1

Southern California News Group
Ron Hasse, President & Publisher
Bill Van Laningham, Vice President, Marketing
Frank Pine, Executive Editor
Tom Moore, Executive Sports Editor
Michele Cardon and Dean Musgrove, Photo Editors

Content packaged by Mojo Media, Inc.
Joe Funk: Editor
Jason Hinman: Creative Director

Contents

INTRODUCTION

The jazz trumpeter Miles Davis is credited with saying that what matters most are not the notes a musician plays, but "the notes you don't play." Vin Scully, born one year after Davis, in 1927, seemed to grasp this concept. His signature call – the trademark of the sportscasting craft – was silence. It was not his call but the crowd's that carried a game's most important moments.

In an interview late in his career with the Dodgers, Scully traced the origin of this practice to his own childhood. Listening to games on the family radio in the Washington Heights section of Manhattan, he remembered lying on the floor, allowing the sound of the crowd to "wash over" him through the speakers. Whether it was Kirk Gibson walking off Dennis Eckersley in Game 1 of the 1988 World Series, or Charlie Culberson walking off the Colorado Rockies in the Dodgers' final home game of 2016, Scully observed his signature pause at the game's critical moment. Silence was not merely integral to the tune Scully sang each night. It was a young boy paying forward a gift he received as a boy, every day of the baseball season, well past his own 88th birthday.

This is why it's so difficult to disentangle Scully the person from Scully the craftsman: His genuine affection for the human condition shone through even when his work reached its most stressful crescendos. Who else can say that? Who else can say they did that for 66 years?

After Scully died on Aug. 2, 2022 at the age of 94, I wrestled with a question about his legacy. Was he so excellent at his craft that he could have done what he did, for as long as he did, if he were a jerk? In the day since he passed, I must have read more than a hundred tributes from colleagues, broadcasting contemporaries, baseball writers, baseball players, and fans. Each memory portrays Scully as exceedingly genuine, a gentleman with rare class. A closer look reveals just how essential his personal excellence was to his professional excellence.

To be clear, while there are many classy men and women in today's broadcast booths, no one was Scully's equal at the craft. In 2016, toward the end of Scully's last season calling Dodger games, I asked MLB commissioner Rob Manfred if there would ever be another one-man booth in baseball. He wasn't sure then, but the answer has revealed itself in time. No one flies solo anymore. Even if the next Vin Scully were born today, he or she would not be the *next Vin Scully.* The structure of modern sports broadcasts would not permit it.

If we're really lucky, we'll get another broadcaster

Vin Scully died on Aug. 2, 2022 at the age of 94, leaving a legacy of masterful storytelling and personal excellence. (Los Angeles Daily News: John McCoy)

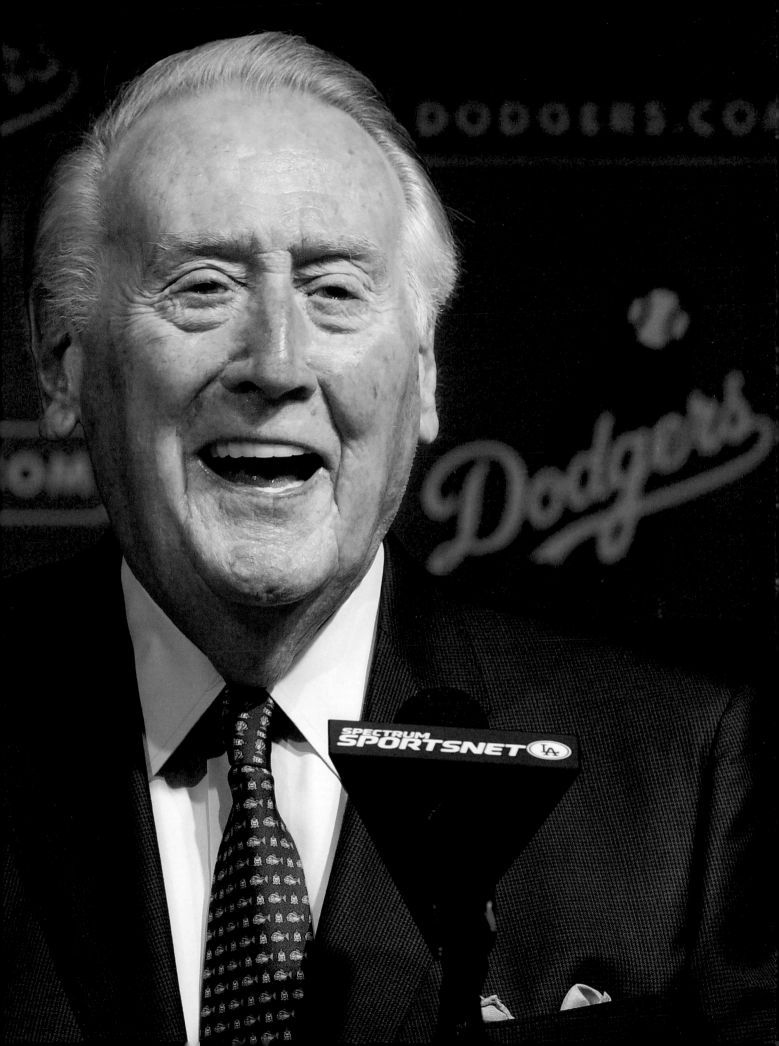

who is an equally astute student of the human condition. Scully had an innate grasp of the universal themes expressed in poetry and literature. He knew, it seemed, that if the great works did not speak to us at some shared level, they would not survive the test of time. Scully was an English major at Fordham University, and his facility for memorizing the classics never seemed to fade, even as Yency Brazoban occasionally became "Brency Yazoban."

Scully also knew exactly when and how to use the more erudite tools in his kit without sounding pedantic, a delicate trick. He successfully balanced his English-major nerdiness with purity and innocence. Cleverly describing a cute baby caught on camera, for example, was not beneath him. What touches a universal emotion more than a cute baby? That's a fantastic prompt for a broadcasting professor.

Of course, when Scully was in college, television and radio were still nascent mediums. No schools of higher learning were devoted to the discipline of sportscasting. There were few professional sportscasters for a student to emulate when Scully joined the Dodgers' broadcast team in 1950, because there were relatively few sportscasters at all. One could argue the classic English major's education Scully received at Fordham would have served him equally well as a broadcaster and a man, in a way that today's emphasis on career-focused training does not.

Scully's gift for storytelling was an offshoot of his first ambition: sports*writing*. (Trust me: his life and ours were both richer for his decision not to become a sportswriter.) There again, Scully's humanity shone through his work. The master storyteller feeds on our proclivity to organize our lives into stories. One

baseball game is a series of discrete innings, an inning a series of discrete at-bats, an at-bat a series of discrete pitches. No matter. Weave a story in between the discrete events, and you have connected them without force, like a needle sewing thread.

Scully used the occasion of the 50th anniversary of the Beatles' penultimate concert to tell the story of their daring escape from Dodger Stadium. He used the occasion of a Madison Bumgarner start to tell the story of how the pitcher once chopped a snake to pieces, only to find a living rabbit among its remains. During a Dodgers-Cardinals game in 2014, Scully spent a half-inning discussing the time St. Louis manager Mike Matheny was the victim of a fly-by bird pooping, keeping him from leaving the University of Michigan to sign a pro contract.

These moments, I think, are the ones that define Scully the craftsman, precisely because they did not occur during pivotal junctures in important games. Years from now, we won't remember the outcome of the Bumgarner-Justin Turner duel from April 2016. (Turner walked.) But we'll remember Bumgarner chopping up a snake to obtain a pet rabbit. When the game mattered, Scully let the crowd do the talking.

Scully never made the big moments about him. He always found a way to make the small moments appeal to us. On Aug. 3, 2022, the New York Yankees, and Houston Astros, and other home teams across Major League Baseball chose the most fitting tribute of all to honor Scully: a moment of silence.

J.P. Hoornstra, MLB Reporter
Southern California News Group

Two Dodgers legends, Vin Scully and Sandy Koufax, shake hands during 2016's Vin Scully Appreciation Day festivities. The voice of Dodger baseball since 1950, Scully narrated the achievements of Koufax and other stars in both Brooklyn and Los Angeles. (Los Angeles Daily News: Hans Gutknecht)

A LEGENDARY BROADCASTER

Vin Scully, Dodgers and Baseball Broadcasting Great, Dies at 94

By Staff and News Service Reports | August 2, 2022

Hall of Fame broadcaster Vin Scully, who called Dodgers games on radio and television for 67 seasons and captivated generations of Southern California baseball fans after the club's 1958 move from Brooklyn to Los Angeles, died Tuesday night. He was 94.

Scully died at his home in Hidden Hills, according to the team, which spoke to family members. No cause of death was provided.

"We have lost an icon," team president and CEO Stan Kasten said in a statement. "His voice will always be heard and etched in all of our minds forever."

Named the No. 1 sportscaster of the 20th century by more than 500 national members of the American Sportscasters Association in 2000, Scully began announcing Dodgers games in 1950 and had the longest continuous service with one team of any major-league broadcaster. Sixty-six years after his debut, Scully called his final Dodger game on Oct. 2, 2016 in San Francisco. A plaque remains on the wall of the visiting broadcast booth inside Oracle Park – where the Dodgers played the Giants on Tuesday night – to commemorate the occasion.

With a mastery of the English language, a near-encyclopedic knowledge of baseball history and an unparalleled story-telling ability, Scully both educated and entertained listeners while receiving nearly every honor the broadcasting industry offers.

"There's not a better storyteller and I think everyone considers him family," Dodgers manager Dave Roberts said. "He was in our living rooms for many generations. He lived a fantastic life, a legacy that will live on forever."

Voted the "most memorable personality" in L.A. Dodgers history by fans in 1976, Scully received a star on the Hollywood Walk of Fame and induction into the broadcast wing of the National Baseball Hall of Fame as the recipient of the Ford Frick Award in 1982.

A four-time winner of the Outstanding Sportscaster Award from the National Sportscasters and Sportswriters Association, Scully was also a 21-time California Sportscaster of the Year. Inducted into the Radio Hall of Fame in 1995, Scully received a Lifetime Achievement Sports Emmy Award from the National Academy of Television Arts and Sciences the following year.

Also a recipient of the George Foster Peabody Award for excellence in broadcasting, Scully covered 12 World Series and six Major League All-Star Games, in addition to football, golf and tennis, for CBS and

Vin Scully acknowledges the Dodger Stadium crowd before a game against the San Francisco Giants in 2016. His wife, Sandi, looks on from the broadcast booth. (Los Angeles Daily News: John McCoy)

NBC, but he will always be linked with the Dodgers. The team honored Scully with the dedication of the "Vin Scully Press Box" at Dodger Stadium in 2001.

Rick Monday interrupted the play-by-play of Tuesday's radio broadcast to deliver the news of Scully's death, choking up as he made the announcement.

"For those of us that were touched by him, listened to him, and learned from him, this is a deep loss," Monday said.

Born Nov. 29, 1927, in the Bronx and raised in New York City, Scully set his sights on being a sports announcer from an early age. He spent two years in the Navy and graduated from Fordham University in 1949, having lettered for two years as a Rams outfielder before turning to broadcasting.

Scully called Fordham baseball, football and basketball games over the school's radio station, and began his professional broadcasting career at WTOP-AM in Washington, D.C. Scully's big break came in 1950, when legendary Dodgers announcer Red Barber and his partner, Connie Desmond, chose Scully to become the third man in the radio booth.

Duplicating Barber's renowned work ethic, by 1954 Scully had become the Dodgers' lead announcer. He called Brooklyn's only World Series championship the following season, and also announced Dodgers World Series victories in Los Angeles in 1959, 1963, 1965, 1981 and 1988.

From the days of Jackie Robinson and Duke Snider in Brooklyn, to the early years in Los Angeles with Sandy Koufax, Don Drysdale and Maury Wills, Scully was at the microphone for nearly every significant moment in Dodgers history since 1950. Scully also called Don Larsen's perfect game for the New York Yankees in the 1956 World Series and Henry Aaron's record-breaking 715th career home run for the Atlanta Braves in 1973.

"This is where I learned baseball. ... I would go to sleep listening to Vin Scully," Angels interim manager Phil Nevin, who grew up in Fullerton, said Tuesday. "My parents let me listen to the radio, Dodger games, before I went to bed. I learned to keep score listening to him. It's a tough day."

Over the course of his career, Scully worked 18 no-hitters, three of which were perfect games, including Koufax's 1965 gem against the Chicago Cubs. His closing words in the final inning of that game are remembered among the greatest play-by-play descriptions of all-time.

"On the scoreboard in right field it is 9:46 p.m. in the City of the Angels, Los Angeles, California," Scully said. "And a crowd of 29,139 just sitting in to see the only pitcher in baseball history to hurl four no-hit, no-run games. He has done it four straight years, and now he caps it: On his fourth no-hitter, he made it a perfect game. And Sandy Koufax, whose name will always remind you of strikeouts, did it with a flurry. He struck out the last six consecutive batters. So when he wrote his name in capital letters in the record books, that 'K' stands out even more than the O-U-F-A-X."

Scully was there for Wills' record-breaking 104 stolen bases in 1962, record scoreless-innings streaks by Drysdale in 1968 and Orel Hershiser 20 years later, and Kirk Gibson's dramatic, pinch-hit home run that won Game 1 of the 1988 World Series against the Oakland A's.

"He meant so much to so many and there will never be another like him," Josh Rawitch, the president of the National Baseball Hall of Fame, wrote on Twitter.

Despite having been associated with the Dodgers seemingly forever, Scully retained a solid sense of objectivity unknown to many revered announcers in the East and Midwest. He also made it a point not

Meagan Newhouse of Echo Park holds up a note she wrote for Vin Scully, joining the many fans who came to Dodger Stadium to honor and celebrate Scully's life. (Los Angeles Daily News: Keith Birmingham)

to get too close to Dodgers players, in order to maintain that perspective.

He opened broadcasts with the familiar greeting, "Hi, everybody, and a very pleasant good evening to you wherever you may be."

Ever gracious both in person and on the air, Scully considered himself merely a conduit between the game and the fans.

"I've always tried to make the players human beings – individuals – rather than wind-up dolls down on the field running around," Scully said. "So I've always searched for the human side of the game, if I can possibly find it. That's the character that I try to paint, the character that the man represents himself. I think that helps, especially when a team is struggling and you have something interesting to say about someone. I think on the other end, a listener might enjoy it."

Although he was paid by the Dodgers, Scully was unafraid to criticize a bad play or a manager's decision, or praise an opponent while spinning stories against a backdrop of routine plays and noteworthy achievements. He always said he wanted to see things with his eyes, not his heart.

"Vin Scully was one of the greatest voices in all of sports. He was a giant of a man, not only as a broadcaster, but as a humanitarian," Kasten said. "He loved people. He loved life. He loved baseball and the Dodgers. And he loved his family. I know he was looking forward to joining the love of his life, Sandi."

Scully was the son of a silk salesman who died of pneumonia when Scully was 7. His mother moved the family to Brooklyn, where the red-haired, blue-eyed Scully grew up playing stickball in the streets.

As a child, Scully would grab a pillow, put it under the family's four-legged radio and lay his head directly under the speaker to hear whatever college football game was on the air. With a snack of saltine crackers and a glass of milk nearby, the boy was transfixed by the crowd's roar that

Dodgers fan Jerry Cienfuegos places a poster he made in honor of Vin Scully at a makeshift memorial in front of Scully's namesake sign at Dodger Stadium. (Los Angeles Daily News: Keith Birmingham)

raised goosebumps. He thought he'd like to call the action himself.

At age 22, he was hired by that CBS radio affiliate in Washington, D.C. In 1953, at age 25, Scully became the youngest person to broadcast a World Series game, a mark that still stands.

Scully moved west with the Dodgers in 1958, and monumental moments in the sport often seemed to find him. When Aaron hit his 715th home run to break Babe Ruth's record in 1974, it was against the Dodgers and, of course, Scully called it.

"A Black man is getting a standing ovation in the Deep South for breaking a record of an all-time baseball idol," Scully told listeners. "What a marvelous moment for baseball."

Scully credited the birth of the transistor radio as "the greatest single break" of his career. Fans had trouble recognizing the lesser players during the Dodgers' first four years in the vast Los Angeles Memorial Coliseum.

"They were 70 or so odd rows away from the action," he said in 2016. "They brought the radio to find out about all the other players and to see what they were trying to see down on the field."

That habit carried over when the team moved to Dodger Stadium in 1962. Fans held radios to their ears, and those not present listened from home or the car, allowing Scully to connect generations of families with his words.

Some of those listeners, like the Angels' Nevin and current Dodgers Justin Turner and Austin Barnes, grew up to become pro ball players and coaches.

"Growing up in L.A., he was the voice I always heard," said Texas Rangers manager Chris Woodward, a former Dodgers coach. "Back when I played my first big league game against the Dodgers, we were playing them in Toronto. The next day, I

was watching my at-bats from that game. The sound was on, and normally the sound isn't on, but I put it on and I heard Vin Scully, talking about me being a hometown guy from California. It meant the world to me. It was a really goosebump moment for me just hearing him say my name."

Scully often said it was best to describe a big play quickly and then be quiet so fans could listen to the pandemonium. After Koufax's perfect game in 1965, Scully went silent for 38 seconds before talking again. He was similarly silent for a time after Gibson's pinch-hit home run to win Game 1 of the 1988 World Series.

Scully's timing was impeccable and he knew exactly how to humanize a moment, such as the way he narrated three-time Cy Young Award winner Clayton Kershaw pitching a no-hitter in 2014 alongside images of Ellen Kershaw, nervously watching her husband from the stands.

"He was the best there ever was," Clayton Kershaw said after Tuesday's game. "Just when you think about the Dodgers, there's a lot of history here and a lot of people that have come through. It's just a storied franchise all the way around. But it almost starts with Vin, honestly. As far as the history of our organization, Vin's been through it all. Just such a special man. I'm grateful and thankful I got to know him as well as I did."

The Dodger Stadium press box was named for Scully in 2001, and the street leading to the stadium's main gate was named in his honor in 2016. That same year he received the Presidential Medal of Freedom from President Barack Obama.

"God has been so good to me to allow me to do what I'm doing," Scully, a devout Catholic who attended mass on Sundays before heading to the ballpark, said before retiring. "A childhood dream that came to pass and then giving me 67 years

Vin Scully waves to the crowd before a 2008 exhibition game against the Boston Red Sox at the Los Angeles Memorial Coliseum. Scully called games at the Coliseum from 1958-1961 during the Dodgers' early years in California. (Los Angeles Daily News: Keith Birmingham)

to enjoy every minute of it. That's a pretty large thanksgiving day for me."

In addition to being the voice of the Dodgers, Scully called play-by-play for NFL games and PGA Tour events as well as calling 25 World Series and 12 All-Star Games. He was NBC's lead baseball announcer from 1983-89, calling memorable moments such as Game 6 of the 1986 World Series.

While being one of the most widely heard broadcasters in the nation, Scully was an intensely private man. Once the baseball season ended, he would disappear. He rarely did personal appearances or sports talk shows. He preferred spending time with his family.

In 1972, his first wife, Joan, died of an accidental overdose of medicine. He was left with three young children. Two years later, he met the woman who would become his second wife, Sandra, at the time a secretary for the NFL's L.A. Rams. She had two young children from a previous marriage, and they combined their families into what Scully once called "my own Brady Bunch."

He said he realized time was the most precious thing in the world and that he wanted to use his time to spend with his loved ones. In the early 1960s, Scully quit smoking with the help of his family. In the shirt pocket where he kept a pack of cigarettes, Scully stuck a family photo. Whenever he felt like he needed a smoke, he pulled out the photo to remind him why he quit. Eight months later, Scully never smoked again.

After retiring in 2016, Scully made just a handful of appearances at Dodger Stadium and his sweet voice was heard narrating an occasional video played during games. Mostly, he was content to stay close to home.

"I just want to be remembered as a good man, an honest man, and one who lived up to his own beliefs," he said in 2016.

Few would dispute he accomplished that.

"I will never know anyone as kind, as gracious, as talented as Vin. Twitter isn't big enough for all the memories, stories, instances of a person who was the best at what he did behind a microphone and who was even a better person than he was a broadcaster," former Dodgers general manager Ned Colletti wrote on Twitter.

In 2020, Scully auctioned off years of his personal memorabilia, which raised more than $2 million. A portion of it was donated to UCLA for ALS research.

"Vin Scully was bigger than baseball. He was the soul of Los Angeles, the undisputed voice of America's pastime, and the narrator of some of the most thrilling moments of our lives. It is impossible to think about the Dodgers without reflecting on Vin's incomparable way with words and the boundless wisdom he shared with generations of fans around the world," Los Angeles Mayor Eric Garcetti said in a statement.

Scully was preceded in death by his second wife, Sandra. She died of complications of ALS at age 76 in 2021. The couple, who were married 47 years, had daughter Catherine together.

Scully leaves four other children (Kevin, Todd, Erin and Kelly), 21 grandchildren and six great-grandchildren. A son, Michael, died in a helicopter crash in 1994. ■

While Vin Scully was no stranger to tragedy in his private life, his broadcasts served as a comforting and familiar presence for generations of baseball fans. (Los Angeles Daily News: Keith Birmingham)

WE'VE LOST A FRIEND

Vin Scully Provided Not Just Baseball Play-by-Play But the Soundtrack of Southern California

By Jim Alexander | August 2, 2022

Southern California lost its voice Tuesday.

Vin Scully was more than just a baseball announcer. He arrived in Los Angeles in 1958, migrating from Brooklyn with the rest of the Dodgers, and he was here because Walter O'Malley resisted the suggestions from the locals to hire an L.A. guy to do the games.

And not only did he become part of our community and part of our culture, but he became synonymous with it. That voice, wishing us a very pleasant good evening, wherever we might be, provided us companionship as well as information.

He became, indeed, a friend to millions of residents of Southern California who had never met him. Those who did, more often than not, were touched by the modesty and humility he displayed, a reminder that the truly great ones don't need to advertise it.

And so it was when the news broke Tuesday night, that Vin had passed away Tuesday at the age of 94, no one wanted to believe it was true.

"We have lost an icon," Dodger president Stan Kasten said in a statement disseminated by the club Tuesday night. "Vin Scully was one of the greatest voices in all of sports. He was a giant of a man, not only as a broadcaster, but as a humanitarian. He loved people. He loved life. He loved baseball and the Dodgers. And he loved his family. His voice will always be heard and etched in all of our minds forever."

So true.

His was an unmistakable voice. He taught us the game, and he led us to buy transistor radios to listen to the radio call when we attended games – first at the Coliseum, where the seats at the top of the bowl were so remote that the players resembled ants in white and gray uniforms, but also after the team had moved to Dodger Stadium in 1962.

"The people needed the radio," he told me years ago. "They didn't need me. They needed whoever was on, and I never forgot that. But the (transistor) radio was the biggest help for us, to make us closer to the fans because they were all listening. And it made you bear down, because if you made a mistake, they were all looking at it."

Vin always maintained it was the message, not the messenger. But consider: While he was still doing seven innings a night on radio, you could sit anywhere in Dodger Stadium and hear those mellifluous tones. When Vin became the main TV voice and his call was simulcast for a couple of innings on radio, there were fewer portable radios in the stands. And since his retirement after the 2016 season, there are hardly any.

Vin would tell the story of how he first became interested in baseball, right down to the date: Oct. 2, 1936, as an 8-year-old redheaded boy walking home from school in New York, seeing the score of a World Series game – YANKEES 18, GIANTS 4 – posted in

City Hall is lit up in Dodger Blue in honor of hall of fame broadcaster Vin Scully.
(Los Angeles Daily News: Keith Birmingham)

the window of a laundry, and becoming a Giants fan because he felt sorry for them.

Yes, he paid it forward. There are multiple generations of boys and girls in Southern California who, 7 and 8 and older, fell in love with baseball via the sound of Vin Scully's voice. You're reading one of them. The year I turned 8, the Dodgers were in a race for the pennant, and Scully and partner Jerry Doggett became constant summer companions, thanks to a transistor radio that, if I remember correctly, was a birthday gift.

That love of baseball was an even greater gift. It has continued to this day, and I'm sure mine is not the only example.

Vin's voice would become the soundtrack of a Southern California summer, be it on the car radio on the commute home when the Dodgers were playing in the East, during a backyard barbeque or pool party, or on one of those transistor radios tucked under the pillow after what was supposed to be bedtime. (All these years later, I'm not admitting anything.)

The best thing? I grew up to become a baseball writer and then a columnist and to share a press box with Scully, who ultimately would have that press box named after him. And I can personally vouch for his graciousness, kindness and humility.

When he referred to us listeners as "friends," it was more true than even he would ever know. Vin was a family friend, and his family was anyone who followed the game, even if they weren't Dodger fans.

And there was this, as well: Red Barber, his mentor, stressed above all that Vin should report, not root. Once, the young Scully – that's what Red called him, in fact, "Young Scully" said that Willie Mays was the best player he'd ever seen. Barber suggested to him that, well, maybe he hadn't been around long enough to make such a definitive statement.

Vin remembered all of those lessons. He realized those nightly broadcasts were advertising for the team he worked for, but he also believed his ability to report, and not root, provided a credibility that, sadly, is too often absent with today's increasingly homerish commentary.

And it's interesting to note – yup, that's a Scully-ism – that in his final season of broadcasts, 2016, a season in which not only visiting broadcasters but players and managers would visit his booth to pay homage, before each game the umpires would look up at the booth and wave. Maybe they appreciated that Vin wouldn't second-guess their every move.

Let us not forget Vin's versatility, either. He worked NFL games for CBS with John Madden and Hank Stram. The famous Joe Montana-to-Dwight Clark NFC title game touchdown at the beginnings of the San Francisco 49ers' dynasty in January of 1982? Vin's call.

He did the Masters for CBS and then golf for NBC, including the Bob Hope Classic in the Coachella Valley. During the '60s he'd do a daytime talk show, and even a game show for a while, "It Takes Two." He became NBC's lead baseball announcer in the 1980s, in addition to his Dodgers duties. Kirk Gibson's home run in 1988? Vin's call.

There's often a thread that runs through life. Vin said Willie Mays was the best player he'd ever seen as a young announcer. Decades later, when he'd seen enough baseball that he could credibly make that call, he still insisted Mays was the best.

The day that Scully called his final game – Oct. 2, 2016, 80 years to the day after seeing that World Series score displayed in that window in New York – Willie Mays joined him in the visitors' broadcast booth at what is now known as Oracle Park, and the plaque commemorating that moment remains in that booth.

And Tuesday night, when the world learned of his passing, the Dodgers were playing in that ballpark.

Rest in peace, Vin. All of Southern California mourns. ∎

While his demeanor was generous and affectionate, Vin Scully believed his ability to report, and not root, lended credibility to his broadcasts. (Los Angeles Daily News: Keith Birmingham)

GRATEFUL

Dodgers Players Cherished Their Time with Vin Scully

By Bill Plunkett | August 2, 2022

At the conclusion of Tuesday night's game at Oracle Park, the San Francisco Giants informed the crowd that Vin Scully had died, offering a brief tribute to the legendary broadcaster on the stadium scoreboard.

It was one last Dodgers-Giants game for Scully to close out.

"You know – he was the Dodgers," Dodgers third baseman Justin Turner said. "Growing up in Southern California, it didn't matter where you were if you heard that voice on the radio or on the TV, you knew the Dodgers were on. I think there are a lot of heavy hearts in here tonight hearing that news – but also very appreciative and grateful that I had the opportunity to come over here and play in this organization and get to know him. And get to consider him a friend.

"It's a tough night."

During his 67 seasons as the Dodgers' broadcaster, Scully called 18 no-hitters. One of the last was Clayton Kershaw's in 2014.

"He was the best that ever was," Kershaw said of Scully. "Just when you think about the Dodgers, there's a lot of history here and there are a lot of people that have come through. It's just a storied franchise all the way around. But it almost starts with Vin, honestly.

"Just as far as the history of our organization, Vin has been through it all. Just such a special man. … Just a tremendous life and legacy that he led and thankful I got to know him."

For players who grew up in Southern California like Turner and Austin Barnes, Scully had already made an impression on them before they reached the big leagues.

"I grew up watching him, listening to Vin," said Barnes, who grew up in Riverside. "The way he called games, it made you feel at home, like he was in your living room. … He's kind of like my childhood, growing up, listening to him call baseball games, just the way he talked about baseball.

"I think he did my debut, I think my first hit. That's something I'll always remember. I got to meet him, talk to him a few times too, just tell him how important he was to me, and how special he was to my childhood and my family, really. I mean, we all grew up listening to Dodger baseball, and listening to games he called. … Almost part of our family."

Turner recalled meeting Scully for the first time as a visiting player with the New York Mets.

"I was with the Mets in town playing the Dodgers and he came down into the visiting clubhouse to say hi," Turner said. "He told me he was a fellow redhead and us redheads have to stick together.

"I thought it was crazy that Vin Scully walked into the clubhouse to find me and say hi to me. That's something I definitely will never forget."

Yasiel Puig was among the former Dodgers who took to social media to voice his appreciation Tuesday night as the news of Scully's passing spread.

Clayton Kershaw praised Vin Scully as "the best that ever was." Kershaw's 2014 no-hitter was just one of 18 no-hit games Scully called during his lengthy career. (Los Angeles Daily News: John McCoy)

"You gave me my Wild Horse name. You gave me love. You hugged me like a father. I will never forget you, my heart is broken. My hand over your family's hearts. Los Angeles, I am sorry I am not there with you today to cry together," Puig wrote on Twitter.

Scully retired following the 2016 season. That final year was filled with pilgrimages by visiting players, coaches and umpires who made their way up to the press box to pose for photos with Scully and thank him for all the memories.

It was a sign of the impact he had on the game.

"He lived obviously a tremendous life. He impacted so many, myself included," Dodgers manager Dave Roberts said. "I think there's an endless amount of people that consider him family, a part of their families. This is a guy that was not only the voice of Dodgers baseball but baseball in general. He was in so many homes. It's a legacy of longevity. It's class. … He was a gentleman. That's something we all should strive to be. He lived a fantastic, fulfilled life.

"What a legacy." ∎

UNMATCHED

Ralph Lawler Espouses Vin Scully's Greatness

By Mirjam Swanson | August 3, 2022

Ralph Lawler used to listen while commuting to work, the longtime voice of the Clippers tuned in to Vin Scully calling Dodgers' spring training games with such style, substance and depth that the basketball broadcaster would shake his head in astonishment.

"He'd be weaving this marvelous story, inning by inning, that was humanizing, and that touched your heart," Lawler recalled. "And I'd think, 'My god. Save that for the World Series!' But he had a story for every moment."

Lawler is a Naismith Basketball Hall of Famer who called Clippers games for 40 seasons before retiring in 2019. And like the rest of us, he was a huge fan of Scully's.

Every broadcaster was, Lawler said.

"It was just so much more than telling us the story of the game," Lawler explained. "And all of us aspired to be able to learn something or do something like Vin, but he was so far above the rest of us, there was no way. He was the best in our business, regardless of the sport. The best there ever was. Nobody is a close second in my mind."

Lawler spoke by phone from Oregon on Tuesday night, shortly after he learned Scully died at his home in the Hidden Hills section of Los Angeles. He was 94.

Scully called Dodgers games for 67 seasons before his retirement in 2016, longer than anyone in professional sports history. With his dulcet delivery,

Scully was a reliable narrator with unparalleled institutional knowledge and a story for every occasion.

"He had," Lawler said, "the ability as a broadcaster to reach in and massage our souls in a way that nobody else in the business has ever come close to doing."

Ten or 15 years ago, Lawler remembers being invited to introduce Scully at a star-studded Screen Actors Guild event at which he was to be honored.

"I was thrilled to death and nervous as could be at the thought of doing it," said Lawler, who remembers spending a great deal of time perfecting a four- or five-minute speech full of "lavish praise and admiration" for that night's honoree.

"I stumbled through it OK and then he got up, stood for 15 minutes, and without a note, without even giving a thought to what he was going to say, he just spoke brilliantly," Lawler remembered. "And I thought, 'Damn! I wish I could do that.'"

But no one could do it the way Scully did.

There was one habit of Scully's that Lawler could mimic, he decided. That notion came a few days after the SAG event, when one of the gracious thank-you notes Scully was famous for found its way to Lawler.

"That was one case where it did teach me a lesson, the value of writing notes to people when they do something kind of nice for you," Lawler said. "So I tried to do that – but still never as well as he did."

Sometimes, Lawler said, it wasn't Scully's words

A video tribute to Vin Scully plays at Dodger stadium following news that the long-time announcer passed away at age 94. (Los Angeles Daily News: David Crane)

that delivered. Every now and then, in the right moments, it was his silence. Take the joyous aftermath of Kirk Gibson's gutsy pinch-hit home run in the 1988 World Series.

As the walk-off homer cleared the outfield fence, Scully announced "she is gone!" And then he paused for a long while before delivering what became one of his most famous lines of on-the-spot poetry: "In a year that has been so improbable, the impossible has happened."

"I have shared this with so many young broadcasters and not-so-young broadcasters, the brilliance of that call," Lawler said. "He waited a minute and seven seconds before speaking, just let the crowd carry the moment.

"Too often, we broadcasters will call a big moment and we think we have to embellish it, but you can't embellish it more than the crowd going crazy while fans are viewing it on television or listening on the radio and going crazy themselves! … he understood that better than anybody: Let the crowd tell the story."

Scully's story, Lawler insisted, "is unmatched."

"He did things that the rest of us could just try to aspire to, but never ever, ever reach," Lawler said. "I just wish I had his words to describe him, because he would do it so much better." ∎

'HE TRANSCENDED BASEBALL'

Vin Scully Was Impactful, Inspiring

By Mirjam Swanson | August 3, 2022

When Fabiola Torres peers at the 20-year-old photograph of her parents standing on either side of Vin Scully, she sees her father, Salvador Torres, fighting back tears.

On Wednesday, all of Southern California was choked up as we remembered Scully, the Dodgers' iconic broadcaster who died on Tuesday night at 94.

Scully is revered not only because he's widely considered the greatest sports broadcaster of all time, but because he was a caring and kind gentleman, and an artist and a teacher whose encyclopedic knowledge incited passion and inspired careers, united communities and brought together families across generations.

And if you look closely, you can see Scully's out-of-the-park impact in that family picture Fabiola Torres spent much of Tuesday night staring at.

It was taken in the early 2000s, when her cousin Jorge Martin – then the Dodgers' director of publications – arranged for her father to meet the man whose voice had for decades been the soundtrack in every family car ride and on every weekend spent working in the garage.

Salvador moved to Van Nuys from Mexico to work in 1956, when he was 12, not knowing English – or baseball. But he loved Vin Scully's voice and he was determined to learn the language, so he began listening to him narrate Dodgers games, enrolling in nightly nine-inning lessons with a velvet-voiced instructor.

"I actually asked my father, 'What word did you learn?'" Fabiola said. "The word he learned? Ambidextrous!"

As used by Scully, ambidextrous became a baseball term to describe switch-hitters who could bat right-handed or left-handed.

Scully would then always add explanations that made sense to Salvador, and those broadcasts became his "gateway to 'American culture,' where he could have a conversation with other fans about baseball and feel included," said Fabiola, an ethnic studies and women's studies teacher at Glendale Community College.

But being an English-speaking baseball fan didn't shield Salvador from harassment and discrimination when he returned from fighting in the Vietnam War, a torment that has stayed with him.

So when Salvador, his earphones draped over his shoulders, met Scully years later, the famous broadcaster didn't just smile for a picture. He hugged Salvador. And he paid him the tribute he was due.

Fan-made tributes to Vin Scully quickly piled up at Dodger Stadium. Scully's dulcet tones provided the soundtrack of summer while entertaining and informing fans across Major League Baseball. (Los Angeles Daily News: Keith Birmingham)

"He said, 'Thank you for your service,'" Fabiola recalled. "And then he said, 'I know you didn't get the respect you deserve.' That's why, if you look closely at that picture, he's holding back tears."

There are a million such Scully stories, and countless listeners for whom his exquisite broadcasts became a template for learning English.

Novelist Susan Straight's 87-year-old mother, Gabrielle Watson, started listening to Scully when she moved from Switzerland to Riverside when she was 19, studying and imitating his pattern of speech so well that soon no one could tell she hadn't grown up in the United States.

Watson's favorite story to tell: The one about the time her daughter covered a game at Dodger Stadium, met Scully and told him her mother loved him.

And then there's Armando Delgado, who moved to East L.A. from Mexico in 1987, when he was 7 or 8. He credits Scully for his English education too.

Because his parents worked evenings, for years he spent that time in his grandfather, Abelardo Delgado, in his tiny bedroom, watching and listening to Dodgers baseball.

"If you want me to watch you, you're gonna watch Dodger games," Abelardo told his grandson. "And you have to sit and listen, because that's how I watch the game."

Young Armando had only one complaint: Abelardo listened to Jaime Jarrín's Spanish call on the radio, but he preferred Scully on the telecast. He and his grandfather would gradually increase the volume on their respective devices until neither could make out anything being said.

Eventually, they agreed to keep the volume on both devices at a moderate level, and so Armando grew up watching games – including Kirk Gibson's pinch-hit walk-off home run in the 1988 World Series – while listening to them called in both Spanish and English.

"I think that's the beauty of the Dodgers," Armando said. "Not just the way they embrace different cultures, with Jackie Robinson and going on to Fernandomania, but the voices they gave us. They gave us such beautiful voices, both in English and Spanish."

And beautiful memories of "heavenly" evenings spent with his grandfather, acutely resonant Tuesday as Armando thought of Scully and Abelardo, who died on Jan. 8.

Bryan Quintas spent Tuesday night thinking of his dad, Silvio, who'd immigrated from Argentina when he was 8 or 9, learned to speak English and love baseball – even more than soccer! – listening to Scully.

Silvio died when Bryan was in college, and so news of Scully's death Tuesday hit him doubly hard: "Vin is just so connected to my dad."

Silvio became a school teacher and modeled baseball fandom for Bryan, who also fell deeply in love with the game, studying baseball almanacs, collecting thousands of baseball cards and spending hours in front of the mirror, mimicking the batting stances that Scully was describing so precisely.

He could do Gary Sheffield, Dave Roberts, and Bryan's favorite, Shawn Green: "Left-handed stance, right foot slightly flared out, hands held high on his pine-tar stained bat …"

As much as Bryan loved those descriptions, he also recognized the respectful way Scully worked, refusing to Anglicize Roberto Clemente's name as other broadcasters did when they called him "Bob," and referring to Wilver Stargell by his preferred actual name.

"He had such a sense of respect for people when he didn't have to," Bryan said. "It wasn't a mandate, there was no social media – and even when social media came alive during the end of his career … he never made a mistake that would even consider anybody to think any less of him."

That genuine decorum also always resonated with Jared Ravich. The senior software engineer for MLB began his career helping freshen up game notes for Scully. As a Dodger-rooting kid living on the East Coast, Ravich used to listen to Scully late at night via

Dodgers manager Dave Roberts points up to Don Sutton and Tommy Lasorda during Vin Scully's 2017 Ring of Honor ceremony. (Los Angeles Daily News: John McCoy)

Armed Forces Radio on a tiny transistor radio.

"Anyone who's lived in L.A. knows when you walk into a room as a total nobody and it's full of people who are well-known, your expectation is never, 'Wow, everyone here is going to be really, really nice to me,'" Ravich said.

"But from Day One in that press box, there were so many extraordinary people there who were super-nice to me. And I think that's why it's the 'Vin Scully Press Box.' Not because he was so great at his job – which, obviously, he was – but because that culture came from him."

From him to everyone tuned in.

"You could just tell the genuine love he had for humanity, and for the fans," Armando Delgado said. "That's one of the things that sticks with me, how much he loved us fans. I remember being able to get that concept at an early age and it made me want to love him back. I was born a big softie, in that I believe in people, but he augmented that in me.

"He transcended baseball; he was life." ∎

WE'LL MISS YOU!

Vin Scully Celebrated in Moving Dodger Stadium Ceremony

By Staff and News Service Reports | August 5, 2022

Dodgers manager Dave Roberts ended a pregame ceremony honoring broadcaster Vin Scully by running the crowd through a chorus of Scully's famous line, "It's time for Dodgers baseball."

Scully, who called Dodgers games for 67 years and retired in 2016, died on Tuesday at age 94.

Behind a beautiful blue sky, there was a moment of silence at Dodger Stadium on Friday for the lovable Scully, followed by a video narrated by Dodgers broadcaster Charley Steiner and accompanied by Israel "IZ" Kamakawiwo'ole's memorable version of "Somewhere Over the Rainbow."

Scully once described a beautiful night as "a cotton candy sky with a canopy of blue." He was the soundtrack of baseball games for generations of Dodgers fans and a masterful storyteller.

"He's the connection, the fabric from the fans to the organization," Roberts told the crowd. "Players change; teams are different. But he was the one constant. And so every night, when you turn on the game, hearing his voice was consistent. And he was the conduit for many to share stories, paint pictures and call a ballgame."

Roberts said Scully wouldn't have liked all the attention.

"Vin, as he's looking down on us right now, well, he hated the spotlight on him," Roberts said. "Well, this is going to be a very uncomfortable moment right now, but he deserves it. Vin was a man of character and integrity and class, a true gentleman. He wasn't just a Dodger. He loved the game of baseball that we all love and care about."

Dodgers and San Diego Padres players stood along the first- and third-base lines during the ceremony.

When Scully called his last game at Dodger Stadium in 2016, he had a banner that hung from his booth that read: "I'll miss you."

Scully told the crowd that he needed them far more than they needed him. On Friday, it was the crowd's turn to send a message to Scully, whose last visit to the venue was on June 9, 2021.

Later during the ceremony, the Dodgers gathered at the mound – where "Vin" was painted – for a photo with the broadcast booth in the background. There was a new banner, unveiled by broadcasters Joe Davis and former Dodger Orel Hershiser, that read, "Vin, we'll miss you."

A bouquet hangs next to the retired Vic Scully mic as the Los Angeles Dodgers celebrate the life of their longtime broadcaster. (Los Angeles Daily News: Keith Birmingham)

Fans gave a standing ovation when the video concluded with a picture of Scully waving from the field with a rainbow behind him.

The umpires gathered at home plate and looked up to the broadcast booth and tipped their caps in honor of Scully. Dodger starter Tony Gonsolin did the same from the mound.

The Dodgers set up tributes throughout the stadium, adding bouquets of flowers wherever there was Scully memorabilia. Some of Scully's most prized possessions – including his World Series rings – will be featured at Dodger Stadium during the next homestand, which begins Aug. 19.

At the stadium entrance, with the welcome sign denoting the address as 1000 Vin Scully Avenue, fans dropped letters, posters, jerseys and thank you signs to the man who became the voice of the team for generations. ∎

Above: Fans left personal messages in a shrine to the recently deceased broadcaster outside Dodger Stadium. (AP Images) Opposite: Broadcasters Orel Hershiser and Joe Davis unveil a banner during a pre-game ceremony to honor the memory of Dodgers announcer Vin Scully. (Los Angeles Daily News: David Crane)

THE LISTENERS WIN WHEN SCULLY IS IN THE BOOTH

Vin Scully is a Treasure, Both to Dodgers Fans and Nationally

By Phil Rosenthal | October 13, 1988

The best pitcher the Dodgers have ever had is not named Drysdale or Koufax, Newcombe or Valenzuela. He is not even named Orel Hershiser. He's in the Hall of Fame but he's still active. He is not overpowering, but his pitches are almost irresistible. There's nothing deceptive about his delivery and he's always effective.

Since the days of the Boys of Summer, Vin Scully has been the voice of summer for Dodgers fans of all ages and incomes. No one does baseball better, and no one sells baseball better. For more than 30 years, it has been a love affair between Vin and the listener - and the guy who works at the ticket window.

While Scully will handle World Series play-by-play for NBC beginning Saturday alongside analyst Joe Garagiola and doesn't mind working with a partner on network telecasts, when it comes to announcing Dodgers games on KABC-AM (790) and KTTV-TV (Channel 11), he prefers to work alone.

"There's a big difference, a philosophical difference to me, when I'm doing a Dodger game as opposed to a network game," said Scully, 60, who did his first national World Series telecast 35 years ago for NBC. "When I'm doing the Dodgers, my prime responsibility is not only to be accurate and informative and, if I'm lucky, even be slightly entertaining. The basic job is to sell - to sell the team, to get the listener to come out and buy a ticket and go to the ballpark - as they say, put fannies in the seats.

"That's basically the objective of the local broadcaster. When I do a game on Saturday (for NBC's "Game of the Week"), I don't have any of that. All I'm doing is the game."

This will mark Scully's 12th World Series telecast, his third with Garagiola, with whom he has handled NBC's "Game of the Week" since 1983. But since the departure of Red Barber, the man who broke in Scully as Dodger announcer in 1950, Scully has been hesitant to work with a partner.

"When I am selling, when I am doing the local team, I don't want anything between me and the listener where I might not be able to sell the listener," Scully said. "I don't want the listener to be listening to me talk to somebody else about the product.

"I want to say to the listener, 'Oh gosh, you should have been out here tonight! What a play that was! Whatever you do, come on by tomorrow. Get out here early. I'll wear a clean shirt. It's going to be a great game. David Cone and blah, blah, blah.' So I'm talking directly to the listener, a man whom I'm trying to sell to come out to the ballpark.

"On the network, I'm not selling. Consequently,

Vin Scully waves to fans before a 2015 game between the Arizona Diamondbacks and the Los Angeles Dodgers. While much of Scully's long career was spent calling Dodgers games for local media, he occasionally took part in national broadcasts, including the memorable 1988 World Series. (Los Angeles Daily News: Keith Birmingham)

I can have a conversation, (with Garagiola) and those at home watch the game and listen to the conversation."

NO BUSH LEAGUER: When Scully was a varsity baseball player at Fordham University he once played against a Yale team that not only had Boston Red Sox bonus baby pitcher named Frank Quinn - who would go on to win a mere nine games in two major-league seasons - but some guy named George Bush.

Of the game, Scully remembers Fordham lost, 2-1.

"I also remember, because I have the box score here at home and I have it laminated on a piece of wood, that the vice president and I shared one thing in common," he said. "We both went oh-for-three."

OUR LIPS ARE SEALED: Scully said it is a myth he can read lips although, through insight and intuition, he seems able to fake it pretty well when someone such as Dodgers manager Tom Lasorda gets into an argument.

"I wish I had that ability because it would be remarkable," Scully said. "I can read a few people, let's put it that way. But I can't read everyone and certain things will deceive you. A mustache, for instance, makes it very difficult unless the player or the coach or the manager is really expressing himself where you can almost see his teeth.

"There are a few players, some managers and some umpires that I can read snippets of the conversation and then, based on what has happened, try to make a logical assumption. But I'm not a lip reader.

"You know, come to think of it, if I could turn the clock back, instead of spending all those years taking Latin, I wish I had taken lip reading." ■

Vin Scully is joined in the Los Angeles Coliseum broadcasting booth by George Allen and Jim Brown ahead of a 1978 Los Angeles Rams game. Scully's versatility afforded him the opportunity to cover football, golf and tennis, but he will always be linked with the Dodgers. (AP Images)

FOLLOWING IN THE FOOTSTEPS OF RED

Red Barber's Influence is Clear When Listening to Vin Scully

By Phil Rosenthal | October 20, 1988

Years from now, when we recall the game-winning, ninth-inning home runs of Mark McGwire and Kirk Gibson in this World Series, it is not the voice of NBC announcer Vin Scully we will remember.

Scully, who paints verbal pictures as well as anyone, realizes the true artist knows when to stop painting. Instead of trying to capture the moment in his own words, he wisely left viewers to hear the roar of the crowd - and the quiet legacy of a man named Red Barber.

"Red was about as influential as any man's influence can be on another man excluding a father-son relationship, and our relationship was almost that close," said Scully, 60, who was 22 years old when he first went to work with Barber, whom he would succeed as voice of the Dodgers and as baseball's preeminent announcer. "He was my mentor. He was, in a sense, my judge and my critic. He was my adviser. He was everything."

Barber, 80, announced his first major-league baseball game in 1934 for the Cincinnati Reds. Five years later, he moved to Brooklyn, where he was voice of the Dodgers for 15 seasons until he left in 1953 under the strain of a deteriorating relationship with team owner Walter O'Malley.

Barber moved to the Bronx, where he did New York Yankees games until Yankees owner Mike Burke fired him in 1966. He lived and worked in Miami for a while then moved with Lylah, his wife of 57 years, to Tallahassee, Fla., where they still reside.

Barber does his weekly broadcasts on National Public Radio's "Morning Edition" each Friday from his home. Ostensibly, he speaks of sports. But he also is free to talk about anything and often does. His on-air conversations with program host Bob Edwards range from current events to the arts to philosophy.

"That's probably why everybody loves Red - not just the hard-core sports fans, but the others, too," said Mark Schramm, a "Morning Edition" staff member. "Sometimes, even Bob doesn't always know what Red's going to talk about."

Today, as 30 years ago, Barber's voice is gentle. His words are precise, the images memorable. Before Barber came along, a pitcher in control wasn't "in the catbird seat," a fight wasn't a "rhubarb." "Hold the phone" wasn't yet part of baseball's vocabulary.

"The biggest thing Red did for me was, No. 1, advise me to be myself, and not to listen to other people," said Scully, who would follow his mentor into

Hall of Fame broadcaster Red Barber, pictured during a 1988 interview, was Vin Scully's early mentor and a significant influence. Barber left the Brooklyn Dodgers' broadcast team in 1953, handing the reins to Scully. (AP Images)

baseball's Hall of Fame. "The second thing was to tell me the required work habits for the job, and I have followed those from Day 1. So he had a tremendous influence on me.

"He impressed upon me the feeling of silence. If you've watched any of the games that we do, I try to call the play as quickly as I possibly can and then shut up and let the crowd roar because, to me, the crowd is the most wonderful thing in the whole world when it's making noise. Things like that. . . . The flavoring, the subtleties, the work habits, oh yeah, they were all more or less ingrained in me because of Red."

The lessons were not always easily learned, however.

"I was a stern taskmaster," Barber said from Florida. "I wanted to be sure he learned, and he learned it right now. We had several differences because he's a pretty stiff-necked fellow. He doesn't bend and he never did.

"I told him from the very start that one thing he could not do was take a drink of any kind of alcohol before he went in the broadcasting booth, that he just couldn't do it. . . . If you make a mistake, people are going to say, 'Well, gee whiz, I guess he was drinking.' "

As Barber remembers it, he arrived at Ebbets Field a few weeks after that initial lecture and found Scully in the press room with a sandwich and a beer. Barber immediately dragged his protege back into the broadcast booth and scolded him. It was only a beer, Scully protested, but Barber would have none of it.

"He got huffy," Barber recalled. "I said, 'We're not going to discuss this anymore, Vinny. If I see you do that again, you're fired.' His face got red. He said, 'You mean it?' I said I certainly did, and, to my knowledge, he's never done it again."

(While Scully does not recall the specific incident, he said he makes it a policy never to drink before a broadcast.)

Barber would not hesitate to correct Scully on the air if he made a mistake in fact or technique. If there was a change in the batting order and Scully didn't have an explanation, he was sent to find one.

A fan looks at memorabilia of Vin Scully as the Los Angeles Dodgers celebrate the life of the Hall of Fame broadcaster. (Los Angeles Daily News: Keith Birmingham)

"I guess I was his guardian, but it didn't take very long," Barber said. "Vinny was better than anyone ever dreamed. He had an immediate talent, he was very intelligent and any time that we corrected him, we never had to do it again. He was a very apt pupil. He was very good. It was just wonderful to see him develop."

It remains Barber's conviction that 75 percent of an announcer's work is done in preparation before he even enters the booth - a lesson not lost on NBC's World Series team of Scully and Joe Garagiola, who announced Yankees games in the '60s with Barber.

Barber doesn't watch or listen to baseball much these days, although he keeps abreast via the morning paper and The Sporting News. To him, covering the sport wasn't an adventure; it was a job. The last thing he said he wants to be is "a prisoner of my television or radio."

The World Series, of course, is different. He watches, if only because he might get asked about it by Edwards on "Morning Edition" this Friday and he would hate to be unprepared. He listens to his former students work and is justifiably pleased. But, he said, there was no way he could have known in 1950 Scully would become the announcer he now is.

"There are two great blessings that God has given human beings," said Barber, once a licensed lay reader in the Episcopal Church. "One is that you can't see the future. Otherwise, how many of us could stand it? The other is that you cannot retain pain. Once you have gone through pain, it's gone. It's vanished. You can remember you had it, but you can't bring it back."

It must have hurt when Dodgers owner O'Malley didn't back him in his fight to get a raise from sponsor Gillette for covering the 1953 World Series, a dispute that gave Scully the first of his dozen World Series telecasts and led to Barber's move to the Yankees the next season.

It must have hurt when Burke fired him as Yankees announcer at least in part because his broadcast partners had grown weary of his lecturing and on- air corrections.

Only the decade before, Barber's same exacting standards had helped shape the man who would replace him as voice of the Dodgers and baseball's leading announcer.

"The biggest thing was he cared," Scully said. "He wanted me to become a good broadcaster. He laid down the guidelines and, if he thought I did something wrong, he told me about it. So I have been, am and will always be deeply indebted to him."

As viewers and listeners, we all should be. For if Scully is in the catbird seat, it is because Barber helped put him there.

"Tell him I'm very proud of him," Barber said. "Tell him I'm listening." ∎

Veteran broadcaster Red Barber maintained that 75 percent of an announcer's work is done in preparation before he even enters the booth, a lesson not lost on Vin Scully. (Los Angeles Daily News: Keith Birmingham)

YEARS OF PREPARATION

Vin Scully Benefits from a Lifetime of Groundwork

By Paola Boivin | May 6, 1990

Aha. It is said that kissing the Blarney stone imparts one the gift of smooth talk. And who, really, is smoother than Vin Scully? Scully was 4-1/2 when he went face to face with the Blarney stone in Ireland's County Cork. He puckered up and in return received some magical gift of prose. He swears that upon his return to the United States from his Irish holiday, he developed an impressive brogue. Makes sense, of course. The Dodgers announcer has always been able to take the best characteristics of his peers and turn them into something special for himself.

He is a product of the announcers he grew up listening to as a youth and the ones, such as Red Barber, he worked with early in his career.

"The thing that always enraptured me about baseball was the roar of the crowd," Scully said. "When I was young, I used to curl up under an old radio, a four-legged monster, and I'd get a pillow and some milk and some saltine crackers.

"And I would curl up under that radio, and I would listen. And when that crowd would roar, it came out of the speakers down on top of me like water out of a shower head. It so excited me."

With moments like that, could Scully have been destined for a career other than broadcasting? Probably not.

He has called Dodgers games since 1950, when he joined Barber on the Brooklyn broadcasting team. He is considered one of the best by his peers, and the expression "paints verbal pictures" often is used in conjunction with his name. He is the master of anecdotes. His voice is a calming influence.

It is these qualities that put Scully into the broadcast wing of baseball's Hall of Fame. And of course, this is Hollywood, so he has a star on the Walk of Fame. The National Sportscasters and Sportswriters Association has named him the nation's outstanding sportscaster four times.

"It begins with his love of baseball," said Ross Porter, who has shared the booth with Scully for 14 years. "I think that comes across to people. He's the greatest anecdote-teller of all time. He has a great grasp of the nuances of the game others might not see.

"He's simply the master of his profession."

Scully, 62, is not one of those announcers who fell into broadcasting by accident, or whose experiences as a professional athlete served as enough qualification.

Vin Scully's sincere love of baseball underscored his talent as an announcer and his gift for storytelling. (Los Angeles Daily News: Keith Birmingham)

He has prepared for this role since those days of curling up under the table listening to the radio.

When he was 8, he turned in a composition to his surprised grade-school nuns titled, "I Want to be a Sports Announcer."

"In those days," Scully said, "shortly after the invention of the wheel, the boys wanted to be policemen, firemen, doctors and Indian chiefs."

There were probably more Indian chiefs than broadcasters during that time. One of the few sporting events the people listened to on the radio was football. Still . . . he had made up his mind.

Scully grew up in a lower-class Brooklyn neighborhood. His widowed mother remarried a quiet, pipe-smoking Englishman when Scully was 5 and neither parent had much interest in sports. But both realized sports were a healthy alternative to life in the streets, so they gently encouraged Scully to head in that direction.

He concentrated on writing but, when he went to Fordham, a Jesuit college, he was introduced to radio. It was a match made in broadcast heaven.

Scully was 22 when he first worked with Barber, the man he would eventually succeed as the voice of the Dodgers. The evolution of broadcasters in the booth during that time included Connie Desmond, Andre Baruch, Al Helfer and Jerry Doggett, who was Scully's partner for 32 years before retiring in 1987.

"Vin's personality has always been easy, friendly and outgoing, and I think that comes across on the air," said Doggett, who lives outside Sacramento. "He has never been conceited or pompous about his position. He's always humble. That inward feeling is felt by people outside."

Scully is a charmer. People stop him in elevators, restaurants, stores. Sometimes they want to talk baseball. Other times they just fawn.

"Vinnie's popularity starts with Vinnie the person," Dodgers executive vice president Fred Claire said. "The fans have such an awareness of Vinnie because he's with

Vin Scully poses for photos following the unveiling of a commemorative bronze plaque, now installed at the entrance of the Los Angeles Coliseum. (Los Angeles Daily News: Keith Birmingham)

them so often. He talks with them almost every day. And the person behind the voice is as good as the voice, and the voice is as good as it can get. It's all genuine.

"With many public figures, of course, the perception is different from the reality. The perception of Vinnie is reality. I have seen him many times on and off the air, and there is only one person there."

It is for this reason, Claire said, that management doesn't interfere with the work of Scully and partners Porter and Don Drysdale. When the Dodgers first moved to Los Angeles from Brooklyn, team owner Peter O'Malley asked Scully if maybe it was time to start rooting for the team because "we're going to be all alone in Southern California."

Scully said he didn't think he could do it. His peers taught him to call it down the middle. But even now he knows some people think he roots, roots, roots for the home team.

"Obviously, it can't be a secret that you work for the Dodgers and you're paid by the Dodgers," he said. "I'm with these players for 162 games, I see the Giants 18 games. So obviously, I know our fellows better, and their wives and their kids, and I'd like to see them do well.

"I'm not a machine, so I'm sure there's a humanness factor involved. The point is that I make an effort to try to be as unbiased and as accurate as I can. If someone said, 'Uh, he's biased,' well, there's no way I can defend it. I can do my best."

Scully has actually been accused of being too critical at times. Last year, former Dodgers outfielder Mike Davis said, "He makes it sound like everything we do is lucky. . . . It would be nice if he pulled for us once."

Says Scully: "He's certainly entitled to his opinion. By the way, Mike was hitting .190 when he said that, and I thought, 'How the heck am I going to give him much credit when he's hitting .190?' "

Scully's name came up when CBS fired Brent Musburger last month and needed a replacement. It surely will happen again in the future. He spent seven years in the national spotlight as an NBC baseball announcer and golf commentator. When NBC lost baseball to CBS in December of 1988, Scully was on a cruise in the Caribbean listening to reggae music.

He didn't take the loss hard. He knew he had the Dodgers to fall back on, and he admits he enjoys the pace of his life these days.

"To be honest, I actually feel more enthusiasm now than I have in several years," Scully said. "I think it's a physical thing, not flying around as much. It's funny. I heard Richard Nixon on the radio the other night . . . and he said, 'I have reached that stage in my life where my Quaker grandmother says you have peace in the core.'

"When I heard that, I said, 'You know, that's how I feel.' I'm totally, completely at peace. It's a lovely feeling."

Scully says, of course, if someone (i.e. a network) wants to talk, he'll listen. But he doesn't expect anything, and he's happy with his life now.

How long will he continue broadcasting?

"I don't know," Scully said. "It's not something I would know how to prepare for. I assume the time will come when I don't want to do it anymore. I've never experienced that, so I don't know what to expect. . . .

"I just know now that when the game is over, I can get in my car and drive back home and think, 'I showed up, I was sober, I was prepared, I gave it my best shot, so relax and drive home.' Not everyone will like it or dislike it. Just do the best you can do." ∎

On the 70th anniversary of Jackie Robinson breaking Major League Baseball's color barrier in 1947, Vin Scully and Rachel Robinson attend the unveiling of a Jackie Robinson statue at Dodger Stadium's Left Field Reserve Plaza. (Los Angeles Daily News: Keith Birmingham)

A MEMORABLE COMPLEMENT

Sandy Koufax's Unforgettable Perfect Game Matched by Vin Scully's Call

By John Strege | September 9, 1990

"**Three times** in his sensational career has Sandy Koufax walked out to the mound to pitch a fateful ninth, where he turned in a no-hitter. But tonight, September the ninth, nineteen hundred and 65, he made the toughest walk of his career, I'm sure. Because through eight innings he has pitched a perfect game. He has struck out 11. He has retired 24 consecutive batters ... "

It was perhaps the best game they'd ever heard, for those who were listening to KFI radio and Vin Scully on this night, 25 years ago.

Sandy Koufax was the story, Scully the storyteller, whose ninth-inning call of Koufax's perfect game was among the most memorable in local sports broadcasting history.

"You can almost taste the pressure now ... Krug must feel it, too, as he backs out ... one and two the count to Chris Krug. It is 9:41 p.m. on September the ninth ... there's 29,000 people in the ball park and a million butterflies ... In the Dodgers' dugout Al Ferrara gets up and walks down near the runway. And it begins to get tough to be a teammate and sit in the dugout and have to watch. Two and two to Chris Krug. Sandy reading signs, into his windup, two-two pitch, fastball got him swinging!"

Scully chose to punctuate his broadcast of the final inning by frequently reminding the listeners of the time and date that history was being made, and he made some history of his own. Scully's words became nearly as memorable as Koufax's deeds.

"The strike two pitch to Joe, fastball swung on and missed, strike three! He is one out away from the promised land ... "

Scully always had made it a practice to mention the date during the ninth inning of a game in which a pitcher has a no-hitter going.

"The reason I do that is to send it to the pitcher so that he has a record for posterity," Scully said last week. "I always put the date just for the player.

"With Sandy, when the ninth inning came, I was just thinking of what else can I do for him that I haven't done in the past. All of a sudden I look up at the clock and it said nine-forty-something. I decided to use the time to record each out."

"Harvey Kuenn is batting for Bob Hendley. The time on the scoreboard is 9:44, the date September the ninth, 1965 ... The two-one pitch to Kuenn, swung on and missed, strike two. ... It is 9:46 p.m., two and two to Harvey Kuenn, one strike away. Sandy into his windup. Here's the pitch, SWUNG ON AND MISSED, A PERFECT GAME! ... On the scoreboard in right field, it is 9:46 p.m., in the city of the Angels, Los Angeles, California, and a crowd of 29,139 just sitting in to see the only pitcher in baseball history to hurl four no-hit, no-run games. He has done it four straight years, and now he caps it on his fourth no-hitter. He made it a perfect game."

"The next day, everybody was telling me how dramatic it was because of the time," he said. "The impact of the time was surprising. I didn't expect that." ∎

Sandy Koufax holds up four baseballs the day after his 1965 perfect game, the fourth and final no-hitter of his illustrious career. (AP Images)

AN EMPTY FEELING

Don Drysdale's Death Hits Vin Scully Hard

By Ken Daley | July 5, 1993

Ross Porter completed the grim task of recording new promos and "sponsored by" credits for the Dodgers' postgame radio program, then walked quietly out of the booth. The old promos and announcements had been replaced.

They were the ones taped with the voice of Don Drysdale, a voice that was stilled by an apparent heart attack early Saturday morning.

"I'm still in shock," Porter said.

He wasn't alone. Vin Scully, the other member of the Dodgers' radio-TV team, also struggled Sunday with the emotional load of the news that at the time was only 16 hours old - that Drysdale, the 56-year-old Hall of Fame pitcher and Dodgers broadcaster since 1988, had been found dead in his hotel room.

"Last night I said, and it was true, that it was the most difficult broadcast I've ever had to do," Scully said. "But despite being emotionally overwhelmed and in shock, there's still a job to do."

Scully, himself a Hall of Famer, distinguished himself with another solid broadcast in which he maintained his composure under some of the most difficult circumstances imaginable. The toughest part, he said, was holding on to the announcement until the eighth inning Saturday, releasing the news only after it

had been confirmed that Drysdale's wife, Ann Meyers, had been notified.

"I was extremely concerned Ann would not get the news the right way," Scully said. "That was the only reason we held back - until we knew for sure she'd been notified."

Scully knew the Dodgers had been unable to reach Meyers, who was at the home of Drysdale's daughter Kelly (from a previous marriage) celebrating a family birthday. His anxiety grew as Drysdale's scheduled middle-innings television shift approached and Meyers still had not been found.

"I began to really worry when the fourth inning came on," Scully said. "I knew if Don wasn't there and Ann was watching, we'd get a call soon. It was a tough burden waiting for the phone to ring, but it didn't ring. That's when I knew Ann must not have been watching."

It was Meyers' mother who first got the news and informed her daughter, said Scully, who took a 20-minute call from Meyers shortly before 4 a.m. (EDT) Sunday.

Aside from his brief announcement, Scully spoke little of the incident during Saturday's final two innings. He taped a pregame segment Sunday in which he reminisced about Drysdale with Dodgers

Vin Scully narrated numerous highlights of Don Drysdale's sensational pitching career. Drysdale later joined Scully in the broadcast booth from 1988 until his death in 1993. (AP Images)

manager Tom Lasorda and pitching coach Ron Perranoski.

"I tried very hard not to be depressed and maudlin about it, because Don wouldn't want it that way," Scully said. "I think your job (as a team announcer) is to provide as much escape from the pains of this world as you can. Part of you wants to cry and just go hide. But part of you says you still have a job to do, just like the players on the field have to play."

Neither Porter nor Scully said Drysdale had complained about not feeling well. The only thing unusual was that he told both he had slept about 13 hours after the team arrived Thursday night, a slumber that left him puzzled.

"But he was joking around and was fine," Porter said. "He came in the booth around the seventh inning (Friday) eating strawberry ice cream and asked me about the postgame interview I was going to do. Then he got up and left, and that was the last I saw of him."

Scully's memories went back to the late 1950s and early 1960s, when Drysdale and Sandy Koufax gave the Dodgers one of the most dominant 1-2 punches in the game.

"Whenever I saw Don back then, he always had half the ballclub with him," Scully said. "He was a magnet for the team. Sandy was the genius, shy and retiring, but Don . . . they just flocked to him.

"Don's baseball life began and ended in Montreal. This is where his career blossomed (as a minor-leaguer in 1955). And this is where he passed on. With Don, it's truly a tragedy because of the young wife and three little children (ages 6, 4 and 4 months) he leaves behind."

Porter said he really only got to know Drysdale after the latter joined the Dodgers' broadcast team in 1988. It's that relationship he will remember.

"He was a good friend of mine," Porter said. "He and I shared a lot. When you're with someone in a booth 200 days a year, you get to know him. And there was many a day we drove around Florida together for exhibition games. He was a wonderful guy.

"For two guys like Scully and Drysdale to be who they are - and be as humble as they are - speaks volumes for both."

Porter paused and looked at the carpet.

"We had a great booth," he said softly. ■

Street signs bearing the names of pitcher Don Drysdale and broadcaster Vin Scully mark paths at the Los Angeles Dodgers' former spring training facility in Vero Beach, Fla. (AP Images)

STILL DELIVERS TRADITION

Despite Constant Change Within Dodgers, Baseball, Vin Scully's Calming Voice Remains

By Jeff Miller | April 5, 1999

He is the only thing as certain as opening day anymore, the only thing more Dodgers than those blue caps, the only part of this game that can still be trusted.

They can abandon Vero Beach. They can have three managers in four months. They can turn the Freeway Series into a one-way, dead-end trip. But there is no way - absolutely zero, none - that the Fox-run Dodgers can mess with this tradition.

Right?

Team president Bob Graziano on Sunday said that, yes, as a matter of fact, Vin Scully can continue broadcasting this team's games for "as long as he can talk."

So, on this annual day of fresh starts, with the Expos and Braves and Twins and Yankees all tied, before the first inning, let's be thankful the Dodgers still have one old habit.

And there he was again, in our living rooms, wishing us "a pleasant Sunday and Happy Easter," and saying those oh-so-warm words: "Hi, everybody, this is Vin Scully."

Never mind that the greeting is redundant, that when we hear his voice there is no need to hear his name, too. Of course, it's Vin Scully. He couldn't be more definitively identified by his fingerprints.

He is what baseball sounds like, as much as a cracking bat, a seventh-inning organ and a guy peddling beer in the bleachers.

There's a reason the producers of The Simpsons mimic Scully's voice whenever they use a baseball broadcaster.

He can sound convincing during the game, when he calls Dodgers starter Darren Dreifort "the wiz from Wichita State," and during the commercial, when he tells us those "boneless golden tradition hams are succulent."

His voice is there when we're put on hold at the team's offices and has been used in video games and movies. His voice is his fastball, and it's still hissing.

Today, Scully will be part of what he calls "the fuss and the feathers" of opening day. He is scheduled to throw out the first pitch to mark the start of his 50th Dodgers season.

He has been with the team longer than the team has been with Los Angeles. When he did his first Dodgers game, Davey Johnson was 7 and there were 16 teams in the major leagues, including the New York Giants and Philadelphia A's.

"I do think about the passage of time," Scully said. "I'm conscious that I've been standing in one place for a while. But I don't dwell on that. I concentrate on the moment."

Standing in one place? That's what Scully keeps reminding us about baseball. See, this game sometimes stands still. These might be the days of the Florida Marlins, a team that bought and sold a World Series winner within one year, but baseball's pace remains much more marathon. It's slow and even, not unlike Scully's descriptions.

And when there is a burst, when the game demands to be noticed, Scully steps aside, surrendering the stage. He has told us about so much history and

Dodgers players greet Vin Scully during a 2016 ceremony commemorating Scully's final season.
(Los Angeles Daily News: Keith Birmingham)

done it with so few words.

"You call the play and get out of the way," he said. "The roar of the crowd is very important. I've never felt I had the words to equal that sound."

The fans selected Scully as the most memorable personality in Los Angeles Dodgers history - 23 years ago. He now has been a Hall of Famer for 17 seasons, the same amount of time he has had a star on the Hollywood Walk of Fame.

But more important than any of that past right now is the future he talked about Sunday. Sure, Scully is slowing down and can only keep appearing on our TVs and in our radios for so long. But, as of opening day 1999, he has not thought much about retiring.

"As long as I'm healthy and enjoying it, why not? " he said. "I still get goose bumps when there's a big hit or a key play. If I didn't get goose bumps, I'd be jaded. But that's not happening."

This game has a way of coldly casting aside those who no longer can keep up. Eddie Murray was a shell

during his last shot. Cecil Fielder has been dumped by three teams since August. And that familiar-looking visitor in the clubhouse Sunday? The one who has bounced around so many camps the past few springs? That was Rob Dibble.

But Scully remains sharp, clear and distinctive. He doesn't mess up the score or the facts and can still turn on all the last names, including the hard, inside fastballs like Mark Grudzielanek.

He has been working on one-year contracts most of his life. Not that the words mean much. According to Dodgers officials, the binding agreement between these parties is much stronger than paper.

That's an important thing to remember today. Because when they peel away so much of the past, when they change a franchise's face and transplant its heart, when they hire a new ace and a new boss and a new boss' boss, at least they can still sound the same.

And there's nothing quite as calming as a familiar voice. ∎

ADEPT AT ADAPTING

Vin Scully Goes with the Flow as Baseball and Culture Change Around Him

By Tom Hoffarth | April 9, 1999

During the past 50 years, those promoters and networks who run baseball have tried to improve the game. It's been an all-out assault on the senses.

The broadcasts use more mini cameras, louder whirling graphics, microphones crammed into anything that's not moving, and ad nauseam replays. The stadiums have become carnival grounds where a game happens to be taking place.

And let's not even get started on Beanie Babies.

But then there's Vin Scully, like a candle, somehow bringing a sense of calm to everything.

You'd think it'd be the other way around: Baseball should move toward preserving its past rather than tweaking its future.

Not really, says Scully, who begins his second half-century not with just the same sport but with the same team. As much as he is a link to the past, he wants to have a future in the game.

"What I've noticed is something that looks like an out-and-out appeal - a drive if you will - to get young fans," the Dodgers' Hall of Fame play-by-play man said. "And today's youngsters, I guess studies have shown they have the attention span of 30 seconds with the combination of push-button radio and remote control. And they love noise - the louder the better.

"And in ballparks all over the country, they play the most raucous rock and roll - even when the park is empty. Naturally, when you're in the marketing business or controlling a network, you know you've got the older people, but you also want the young ones. So you make it loud - crash, boom, bam. . .."

Scully paused as only Scully can do - to make the story better and to stop himself from sounding like some crotchety baseball fan pining for the good old days. He broke into a huge smile.

"So if that's what kids want and it brings young fans in, go to it. And I just go with the flow. Maybe I don't like all the pizzaz. But I understand, or at least I think I do. I would feel much worse if they changed the game. But the packaging, the wrapping . . . that's another story.

"I guess the secret for me has been to accept the change. Yesterday is gone. Just like all those years at Vero Beach (the Dodgers' spring-training site in Florida). That's where I connect to this team so much more than in any other way. But it's yesterday. They can always move the pictures to a new place. You have to keep adjusting to change."

In the beginning, sharing a press-box microphone with Red Barber and Connie Desmond, there was this 22-year-old still living with his mom, stepdad and sister

Allan Roth, a statistician of the Los Angeles Dodgers, sits in the booth with broadcaster Vin Scully in 1963 in Los Angeles. Despite predating the team's move westward, Scully always managed to adapt to a changing game. (AP Images)

in a fifth-floor walk-up apartment in the Bronx. He was a year out of Fordham University (also in that borough).

Scully had been hired just months earlier by Branch Rickey to replace Ernie Harwell, who moved across town to call games for the New York Giants. Barber recommended Scully based on a Maryland-Boston College football game Vin did for CBS Radio while freezing on the roof of Fenway Park.

On April 18, 1950, the Brooklyn Dodgers opened the season with a 9-1 loss at Ebbets Field to the Philadelphia Phillies. Robin Roberts pitched a complete game against Don Newcombe, who came out after the second inning. Jackie Robinson batted cleanup and played second base.

Scully admits he remembers nothing from the game he broadcast over WHM in New York.

"I was thoroughly intimidated and scared to death," is the best his mind can do for him. "My attitude then was I'd go to ballpark like a bad hitter who was going up to the plate saying, 'I don't want to strike out,' rather than 'Get a base hit.' I was thinking, 'God, please don't let me make a mistake.'"

Early in his career, Scully was as much a TV broadcaster as a radio man. In 1950, the Dodgers did all 77 home games for WPIX-Channel 11. A few seasons later, they added 25 road games.

And after Game 6 of the 1954 World Series, Scully found himself really on his own - Barber, upset over how little money he received for doing the Series, went to work for the New York Yankees with Mel Allen.

Then came the move to Los Angeles in '58 and the boom of transistor radios from fans who brought them to games at the Coliseum to help them follow what was going on way down on the field. It became Scully's medium.

He not only introduced an entire city to big-league baseball, but he had a captive audience - so much so that when the team moved over to Dodger Stadium, owner Walter O'Malley didn't put any home games on TV for years.

Scully has come a long way to his 50th season - a family-owned team now a Fox-owned team that will be on

Dodgers fans sport shirts honoring Hall of Fame broadcaster Vin Scully, as beloved in 2022 as he was during his 67 years calling games in Brooklyn and Los Angeles. (Los Angeles Daily News: Keith Birmingham)

TV home and away more than 130 times in 1999. Scully will do as many of those games as he can handle, and you'll hear less and less of him on the radio.

That's progress?

It's an adjustment that others of his era have had to make, moving from radio, which was the dominant medium, to another, television, to the cusp of another, the Internet, to broadcast the sport.

Like everyone, Scully, 72, marvels at how octogenarian Chick Hearn has made it through it all to be doing games for the Lakers in his 38th year with the team.

"He obviously loves it and it obviously makes him happy," Scully said of Hearn, trying to figure out his secret for longevity.

"I've always felt a man's job almost - almost - is the man. There's so-and-so the doctor, or the lawyer . . . it's so much a part of you. I think when you give it up, you lose something maybe not in the public eye, but your own self-worth is challenged.

"I know I don't like the idea of playing golf every day. I found that out during the strike of '94. That's when I knew I couldn't just walk away from this."

With no guarantee of calling Dodgers games for another 50 years, what will Scully be doing five or 10 years from now? His current contract keeps him here three more years, through 2001.

"After that, it's a question. . .. I mean, as long as I enjoy it and I'm healthy enough to do the job, the enthusiasm is honest, the crowd roar brings the goose bumps, I'll probably keep doing it.

"I'd hate to turn the engine off after all these years."

Scully paused again.

"It's that old story: If you want to make God smile, tell him your plans." ∎

Fans gather to remember Vin Scully at the Welcome to Dodger Stadium sign along Vin Scully Avenue. (Los Angeles Daily News: Keith Birmingham)

BRINGING US BACK

Scully's Words Give Comfort in the Wake of Tragedy

By Tom Hoffarth | September 21, 2001

He says it was nothing more than "a very ordinary person asked to say something at a very difficult time."

But for heaven's sake, L.A. sports fans would be lost without the comforting words of Vin Scully to cling to this week.

In a brief, poignant introduction to the Dodgers-Padres telecast Monday, Scully established a tone that started very solemn but slowly unfolded, pitch by pitch, into a gathering of people watching something that was worth appreciating again.

"The mood was down, but at the same time, people there wanted to see a game," Scully said Thursday morning. "It was interesting. I'm no expert in psychology, but as the game went along, you could see people were more into it. That was great to see.

"Even last night, there was an extra special kick to 'Take Mc Out to the Ball Game,' with people finally smiling and laughing. I'm finally noticing a lighter mood in the park."

The tragedies in New York and Washington didn't escape Scully's family circle. His nephew, Dan McLaughlin, worked as an attorney with an office in one of the Twin Towers on the 52nd floor, and normally would have been at his desk at 8:30 a.m. that Tuesday. But because of a primary election going on in the state that day, he decided to register to vote on the way to work and avoided the initial calamity.

"He was very fortunate," said Scully about his sister's son. "For anyone who had anyone in that part of New York, it definitely brought it closer to home."

Through several personal tragedies, Scully says his faith in God is where he draws his strength — "Fortunately it hasn't wavered and hopefully it never will" — and it won't cause him to hesitate before he boards a plane again next week when the Dodgers go on the road for the final part of the regular season.

He hasn't had to catch himself from using war terms during the telecasts he's done this week, noting "the battle isn't with semantics now, it's a lot to do with everything else."

And to compare it to anything that's happened in his professional career, he relates it closer to the 1963 assassination of President Kennedy because of the TV impact it had on the nation.

"When Pearl Harbor occurred (in 1941), all we had was radio, and you had to wait until Monday to see pictures, and then maybe in a week, you went to the movies to see newsreels," said the 72-year-old Scully.

"We can only be addicted so much to depressing television. When President Kennedy was assassinated, the country wouldn't let go of the mood that TV helped create. All of a sudden, we were no longer naive to assassinations. We hadn't had anyone assassinated in this country since Abraham Lincoln. That really took the wind out of our sails.

Fans react as a giant American flag is displayed on the field prior to the start of action between the Dodgers and the Padres in Los Angeles on Sept. 17, 2001. Baseball returned to the field nearly a week after terrorism halted play. (AP Images)

"Now, after a week of everyone watching all the awful things happening, time after time, we needed something after all the self-confidence I think we lost. This is a country that defeated the German army and air corps, the Italian army and the Japanese armies and air corps in our time, but 19 people brought us to our knees. It was a very sobering thought.

"I guess America's strength is resilient and baseball has been helping to inspire Americans to play again. I think we're doing that."

And so has Scully's voice, bringing us back.

Especially with Monday's introduction.

"I'm not an official, just an announcer. I'm not making some great proclamation," Scully said. "After doing a lot of soul searching, I just said what I felt and what was in my heart.

"The nicest thing I've had people say to me is, 'When I hear your voice, I think of my dad barbecuing in the backyard,' or 'I remember a summer vacation.' It's nice to be considered a bridge to a family memory.

"If it helps to bridge a nightmare into some normalcy, I'm pleased to serve as that bridge." ■

SPEAKING JUST TO YOU

Vin Scully's Rules for Announcing

By Paul Oberjuerge | July 1, 2007

It's 50 years now that Vin Scully has been the best friend we've never met.

Five decades that he has invited us to "pull up a chair" and share with him the simple joy of another Dodgers baseball game.

Half a century that his relentless goodwill, endless wonderment and lyric cadences have alternately soothed and thrilled millions of Southern California baseball fans.

Players come and go, managers are hired and fired, owners buy and sell. Scully has been the one constant in the history of Los Angeles Dodgers baseball and, without question, the Most Valuable Person of a massively successful franchise.

"It could have been someone else, very easily, who arrived here around the same time under the same circumstances," Scully said, "and it would have been his good fortune instead of mine."

Normally, only a churl would contradict Vin Scully. But he is wrong about that "someone else" business.

It could not have been someone else.

Someone else wouldn't have the gravitas to make every Dodgers game a significant event by his mere presence in the broadcast booth.

Someone else wouldn't have the steadfast decency and manifest honesty to attract so many and repel so few.

Someone else wouldn't have been so literary with so little pretense, so personable with so little ego.

Someone else would not have missed "maybe five?" games that he was scheduled to work in 50 seasons.

Scully is arguably Los Angeles's greatest living treasure. He is the one intellectual concept that a fractured, fractious region can agree upon. There is no measurable dissent: He makes Los Angeles a better place to live.

Vin Scully never planned to be anyone but himself, but the decisions he made throughout his broadcast career—and his Los Angeles history dates to the club's April 15, 1958, debut, making this his 50th season—propelled him to the peak of his profession and the zenith of regional popularity.

As an announcer, he set these rules for himself:

Be a journalist, not a cheerleader. Scully's credibility pivots on the clear distinction he draws between broadcaster and team. Even at critical moments (the ninth inning of Sandy Koufax's 1965 perfect game is a good example), his reportorial rigor trumps his rooting interest.

Make broadcasting a personal experience. In Scully's mind, he has an audience of one, and listeners seem to revel in the attention. "I've always felt that I was talking to one person," he said. "But

Vin Scully set rules as an announcer for himself that kept him at the top of his game for decades. (Los Angeles Daily News: Hans Gutknecht)

I've never envisioned who that one person is."

Turn athletes into human beings. From his days (1950) as the 23-year-old boy wonder of the Brooklyn Dodgers' broadcast booth, Scully has emphasized the personal over the statistical. The anecdotes he exhaustively collects and weaves into the game narrative are his calling card—and his ticket to the Hall of Fame.

Describe but don't judge. Scully can be clinically precise, but he never condemns and rarely criticizes. He leaves that to the audience and other media.

Don't follow fads. Scully never uses jargon. A home run is a home run; it never will be "going yard." "I'm still very much old-fashioned," he said, "a purist, whatever."

Never forget the event is about the play, not the playwright. Everyone who has listened to Vin Scully feels as if he or she knows him. In point of fact, he reveals almost nothing of his personal life. (We never knew his first wife died in 1972, or that he remarried in 1973 and has four children and two stepchildren, and that his oldest son died in a 1994 helicopter crash.)

To be certain, Scully brings gifts to the workplace. A pleasant, calming voice. A formidable intellect. Quick wit. A prodigious memory.

But lots of announcers are smart guys with pleasing baritones and a gift for gab and quick recall. None of them is Vin Scully.

It is amazing and a little alarming that Scully will be 80 years old in November.

He looks like a much younger man and seems to have the energy of one — even as he concedes he may have lost a step from his professional prime.

"I think as players slow up, as their eye-hand coordination slows up, I think as a play-by-play announcer, the mind and the tongue might not always be as sharp as it was," he said. "So I think I would be less than honest to say I'm as sharp.

"I still think I do a reasonably good game."

He is keenly aware that sickness or injury could have curtailed his career. "I'm not really affected by anything that's happened to me except an overwhelming feeling of thanksgiving to God to a) give me the job at an early age, b) to allow me to keep it so long and to keep my health all these years. Really, in retrospect that's the bottom line, and I'll never, ever get over that feeling."

Scully insists he doesn't feel like a celebrity but concedes he is often treated like one. And you may be pleased to learn he likes you as much as you like him.

"I like (listeners) to think of me as a friend," he said. "One of the nicest residual effects of this job is to have people say to me, 'You know, when I hear your voice, I think of summer nights with my dad in the backyard and a barbecue,' or 'I can remember fishing with Dad,' or 'I remember Mom and Dad taking me somewhere and I heard the game,' and it's a nice feeling. I really do love that."

Fifty years in, the Dodgers without Scully seems almost impossible to imagine. But it has to end someday, as awful as that day will be.

He has a contract through 2008 (and earns about $3 million per season) and seems willing to continue beyond then with his reduced (generally, no games east of Colorado) schedule. He said the 1994 baseball strike, and the enforced idleness, bored and startled him.

He began by playing golf, then moved on to having lunch with the guys, "And all of a sudden, I was spending an inordinate amount of time in the hardware store ... and all of a sudden, I thought 'Oh, my gosh, imagine if this was it?' ... I don't know if I can handle it."

Not that he assumes eternal health. "One of my favorite expressions is, 'If you want to make God smile, tell him your plans,'" Scully said. "Come 2008, ... we'll see."

And Los Angeles, of course, will be rooting for years and years more for its hail-fellow-never-met. ∎

Dodgers manager Dave Roberts is one of many individuals that Vin Scully covered as both a player and a coach. (Los Angeles Daily News: Keith Birmingham)

LONGEVITY, PREDICTABILITY, EMPATHY

The Enduring Qualities of Vin Scully

By Kevin Modesti | September 6, 2011

Vin Scully announced last week that he plans to broadcast Dodgers games on television and radio again next season. Los Angeles baseball fans reacted with predictable joy and relief. Scully may be L.A.'s most admired figure, whatever that says about the city.

It's not just that Scully is astonishingly good at what he does, at age 83.

It's also that he epitomizes qualities which used to be celebrated but are actually discouraged in today's VIPs — including a quality that, for one group of leaders, is prohibited by law.

Longevity. Scully has been calling the play-by-play of Brooklyn and L.A. Dodgers games for 62 years. Though he has done other sports and other TV, it is decades of Dodgers games that define him.

Who does one job for a whole career anymore? The athletes whose activities Scully narrates must hop from one franchise to another, or threaten to hop, to get the biggest contracts. Entertainers are told not to do the same thing for too long before they re-invent themselves. And politicians are forced by the term-limit laws in vogue since the 1990s to abandon many offices even if they're effective and popular.

Good thing nobody in Dodgers management ever looked at Scully and applied term-limits rationale to him: It would be nice for the Dodgers to have a new voice every few years, just to freshen things up! There's a risk the old guy will get complacent! So many years

on the club's payroll could skew his judgment!

People come along all the time who do something with Vin Scully-like brilliance. Before long, the world tells them to do something else.

Predictability. Scully has become an icon by doing exactly what is expected of him, no less but also no more.

That is not in the modern fame-seeker's handbook, which promotes the element of surprise — keep 'em guessing about whether you're running for president, go on TV in your male alter-ego, keep secret the defining events of your life until a publisher pays you to spring it on the world.

Fans from other cities used to be disappointed when they first heard Scully. He was so often described as baseball's bard, they imagined him emitting a steady stream of poetic word-pictures and comedy. In fact, the best thing about Scully is that he always does the simplest thing — he says what is happening on the field, a shockingly rare skill for sportscasters.

Recently, I tuned in the late innings of a close game on the radio. The bases were loaded with one out. The broadcaster — not Scully — dropped into a portentous growl as he described a fly ball to center field. With great flair, the man said the ball was caught, and a runner had scored. And he told listeners nothing else: Did the runner trot home or sprint? Did he slide in ahead of the throw? Was there a throw?

Vin Scully would tell us, because it's the most basic requirement of his job.

Vin Scully is an expert at capturing the attention of an audience, be It on a broadcast or in a pool of reporters. (Los Angeles Daily News: Keith Birmingham)

The only way his announcement about next season could have received more attention is if he'd made it while wearing a cube on his head.

Empathy. Next to the word "snarky" in the dictionary is a picture of everybody except Vin.

In a culture of reality TV, news media and politics increasingly based on making fun of others' failings — from the "Worst Person in the World" on up — Scully is unfailingly encouraging and upbeat. Even a .170 hitter for the San Francisco Giants has a mother. And here's a little story about her …

He has spent 62 years around ballplayers (not to mention ballclub owners). He has known all the behind-the-scenes gossip. Think of all the bad stuff that must pop into his mind. Yet none of it comes out on microphone. None of it comes out in a book or an interview.

This guy will never make it on cable.

Baseball fans are happy that the voice of the Dodgers plans to stick around for at least one more year. They say when he retires, it will be the end of an era. How right they are.

If there never is another Vin Scully, it might be because the world won't allow it. ■

SHANGRI-L.A.

'You Leave It, and Your Real Age Catches Up With You.'

By Tom Hoffarth | November 28, 2014

O n my mental iPod/way-back machine, Vin Scully probably gets the most search and playback requests these days.

You know how the marvelous mind works. You hear something, and it reminds you of something else. You hit memory mode and hope the audio files arranged in this neurotransmitting system are uploaded to the right version.

So now we've hit pause, because Father Time has called another timeout.

The Dodgers' Hall of Fame broadcaster and city of Los Angeles treasure turns 87 on Saturday. The kinetic brain energy kicks into motion again. Hopefully, the batteries are charged.

There's that phrase Scully turned during Clayton Kershaw's no-hitter from last season, telling people it might be time to call up a friend to let them know some history is in the making. Then he corrects himself, saying that texting is probably the best way to go about it these days.

The story he told about Indians climbing mountains to see the sea during his 1982 Hall of Fame induction speech still brings goosebumps.

Then there's the way he ad-libbed on a movie soundtrack for a game that never really happened —

describing how Kevin Costner, as Billy Chapel, struggles to throw a perfect game in "For Love of the Game."

The voice of Vin. The sound of Scully.

Hear what I'm saying?

"Well, it is a little unbelievable because God has been so good and given me good health — and he did it through my mom, who lived to be 97, so certainly the biggest reason how I got this far is because of her genes," Scully said Friday morning when asked what it sounded like to be on the cusp of another birthday.

Thankfully, we can Google up a YouTube clip to restore our DNA data plan. Scully lives perpetually in a digital cloud, a voice from the video-streaming heavens. If only someone had the tapes of when he first started calling games in Brooklyn some 65 years ago.

I listen to Scully converse casually on the phone, and it's a reminder again that, frankly, my hearing isn't what it used to be.

Decades of trying to work around insufferable tinnitus in the left ear has resulted in more than a 50-percent loss of decipherable sound from that side, and it worsens by the year. Hearing aids only amplify the non-stop ringing.

So the right ear gets overtaxed. Someone like me who loves to listen rather than talk — it's why God

Vin Scully acknowledges the fans as he arrives to throw the ceremonial first pitch before the home opener in Los Angeles between the Dodgers and the Giants on April 4, 2014. (AP Images)

gave us two ears and one mouth, I'm reminded — wonders when the other senses will overcompensate as this nonsense continues.

It's more difficult to sit and work in an indoor sports arena where the bass-heavy music over the more sophisticated speaker systems permeates membranes and causes more permanent damage. I'm in constant preservation mode against loudness. My only recourse is that a sense of humor offsets a sense of longing for what's never coming back.

I hope to someday to hear the pitch perfect of a grandchild's first words as clearly as Scully's perfect description of a Kershaw pitch.

The voice of Vin. The sound of Scully.

From his lips to my one good ear, he makes perfect sense of what sense he appreciates most at this stage in the game.

"For me, the sense of sight has to rank No. 1," he said. "Not only because there's this great big world to look at, but when you do want to beat a hasty retreat from it, there's always a good book you can find to read."

Scully has spent time with generations on holidays and birthdays, and he says he can envision them beyond his mind's eye. He's protective of his voice, sure. But his royal blue eyes start the process of what he's about to tell us. And it's imperative that we listen.

He explains a resistance he has when it comes to imagining how he'd see himself in a mirror if he didn't have baseball as part of his life today, just a few months away from starting his 66th season with the Dodgers.

"Remember the book by James Hilton called 'Shangri-La,'" Scully begins, referring to the 1933 novel that was made into a Frank Capra movie a short time later called "Lost Horizon" starring Ronald Coleman and Margo Albert.

"This plane crashes into the Himalayas of Nepal, and the survivors are met by Sherpa guides who take them off the mountain, during a terrible blizzard. The next thing you know they're in the most beautiful valley in the whole world, absolutely magnificent — it's Shangri-La.

"So now one of the survivors falls in love with this gorgeous girl in the valley. Finally, there comes a point when the survivors are restless and want to be rescued. So when they are rescued, this man decides to leave but he wants to take this woman back to civilization.

"When he announces his plan, the High Lama says that he can't take her away from Shangri-La. He warns him that she is a lot older than she looks. She has only managed to stay her youthful age because she has lived in this valley for so long, and if she leaves, she'll revert to her real age.

"But the man takes her anyway. And in the movie, there's the scene where they're leaving the valley, all dressed in winter clothes. The man is carrying the woman out on his shoulder. And then the camera zooms in on her. From under her hood, you can now see her face — and she looks to be 150 years old."

Scully pauses for effect, and reflection.

The voice of Vin. The sound of Scully. The eyes have it. I'm listening even more intently.

"I've often thought that when the time comes to leave baseball, I'll have lived this sheltered, lovely existence where grown men leave a child's game. It's like Shangri-La. You leave it, and your real age catches up with you."

In Shangri-L.A., it's always time for Dodger baseball with Scully. No matter what the calendar says.

See what I'm saying? ■

For decades Dodgers fans brought radios into the stadium so they could listen to Vin Scully's brilliance while they watched the game. (AP Images).

JUST A LITTLE LONGER

Vin Scully Enchanted Millions, Including One Future Reporter

By Todd Harmonson | August 30, 2015

She knew the punishment for her 10-year-old son required an impact, so she made him hurt. She took away Vin Scully.

Never mind that the Dodgers were lousy in 1979. Her son listened to every game, developing an appreciation for both the finer points of baseball and the word pictures painted nightly by the master artist.

Then he got busted at school — something about foul language and forgery in the fourth grade — and his mother confiscated his transistor.

Two weeks of misery and relying solely on — gasp — a newspaper for information seemed like an eternity to the son who knew he was being deprived of greatness. Then Scully kept going longer and doing his job better than anyone thought possible.

And, despite all attempts by satellite and cable providers, no one could take Scully away until he was ready.

He almost is.

Scully revealed recently that next season, his 67th, will be his final one as the Dodgers' announcer and the voice of all the generations who ever spent a pleasant good evening with him.

Nearly 18 years after the elementary school scofflaw learned his lesson — don't get caught — he was invited by the man himself to pull up a chair.

The reporter and the legend agreed to meet in Scully's time off the air during a Freeway Series game at whatever the Angels called their stadium in March 1997. The 50th anniversary of Jackie Robinson breaking baseball's color barrier was approaching, and the reporter wanted to hear from someone who knew Robinson.

Once the interview was over, Scully asked the reporter if he wanted to watch some of the game with him in the media dining room.

In the nanosecond it took to casually say, "Sure, why not?" the reporter had time to remember being introduced to the voice of his childhood soundtrack by his baseball-loving grandfather, the one who cherished Scully's calls of Wally Moon's "moon shots" and had a Moon baseball card slipped in his casket by his oldest grandson.

And the next day, the reporter called his mother to share the experience with her and remind her of the long-ago punishment.

"You deserved three weeks without your radio, but I just couldn't do that to you," she said.

Just as he steadily avoids any opportunity to meet the favorite players from his childhood – sorry, Ron Cey and Fernando Valenzuela, he doesn't want the perception formed in the glorious October of 1981 tainted in any way – he never wanted to spend too much time with Scully.

A few brief meetings and countless hours listening were all he needed.

The relationship between Vin Scully and Dodgers fans is as special as any in baseball or sports history. (Los Angeles Daily News: Stephen Carr)

Now the reporter is an editor whose passion for the Dodgers long ago was Foxed into submission. But he still turns on the radio whenever possible to listen to one of the only voices he has heard throughout his life, a voice that remains even as his late parents' have faded.

It's the voice of an erudite friend who delivers the romance and drama of a sport that has a leisurely pace that is the antidote to modern-day madness.

And it is the voice of comfort and reassurance, a reminder that some things do not have to change.

They finally will at the end of next season, a campaign that could include the most significant increase in Dodger fans since their move to L.A. with a red-headed poet laureate at the microphone.

They'll cheer for a deep run into October that will keep Scully on the air just a little longer, defying time and logic once more to provide the melodic accompaniment to a few more memories of the fall. ∎

VIN SCULLY AVENUE

City Council Votes to Rename Path to Dodger Stadium

By David Montero | April 11, 2016

The way to get to the Dodgers has always been through Vin Scully. The city of Los Angeles literally made that so Monday.

Elysian Park Avenue street signs came down and city workers replaced them in the morning with blue Vin Scully Avenue signs at the intersections of Sunset Boulevard and, further up the hill toward Dodger Stadium, Lilac Place. The honor was bestowed on the longtime Hall of Fame broadcaster when the City Council voted unanimously to rename the stretch of road.

Scully stood at a podium on his own avenue and said he was "overwhelmed" by the gesture that has come in the final year of his 67th year as the Dodgers announcer.

"I can't believe you're all here," he said.

A few hundred fans — some hoisting pictures and bobbleheads of the 88-year-old broadcaster — cheered, laughed and chanted his name as Scully told them what he was going to miss the most.

"The roar of the crowd," Scully said. "Which is really what I'm saying today. I don't know you, and I miss you, believe me — each and every one of you."

City Councilman Gil Cedillo, whose district includes Dodger Stadium, had been key in pushing to make the name change, with Scully joking at the ceremony that the council, "despite my no, overrode it."

Cedillo said Scully brought the city together, telling how he used to listen to the radio with an earpiece.

Then he heard how fellow council members had similar Scully experiences.

"This is what you did," Cedillo said. "You united our city and the various communities and various generations."

Charlie Steiner, who also calls Dodger games, said the influence of Scully on him was immediate.

"You had me at, 'Hi everybody and a very pleasant good afternoon wherever you may be,'" Steiner said. "I happened to be in my mom's kitchen."

Sam Kane, a 67-year-old Woodland Hills resident, said he can barely consider the idea of a season without Scully and, because it was his last season as the team's broadcaster, had to be present for the ceremony.

It all felt bittersweet.

"I really wanted to be a part of history," Kane said. "He has been the communicator of history."

Some have opposed the street change name, however.

At the City Council meeting, some residents from the Echo Park and Elysian neighborhoods said the change was a greater move toward gentrification of the area.

Luzia Padilla, who lives in the neighborhood, came to the ceremony and said she feared the street name was part of a larger plan to replace homes with a "restaurant row" and turn the newly named road into something similar to Universal City Walk: heavy on shopping and dining and light on housing.

"I love Vin Scully, but I don't love this action," Padilla said.

Vin Scully and Stan Kasten, President and CEO of the Dodgers, unveil a sign of Scully's namesake at the entrance to Dodger Stadium on April 11, 2016. The Los Angeles City Council officially renamed Elysian Park Avenue as Vin Scully Avenue. (AP Images)

Scully began with the Dodgers in New York before the team moved to the Los Angeles Memorial Coliseum in 1958. They started at Dodger Stadium in 1962. Dodger games became famous for fans sitting in the stadium listening to Scully on radios from their seats.

Los Angeles Mayor Eric Garcetti said there was a practical reason for that, which was explained to him by his father.

"I said, 'Dad, we're at the game. Why are they listening to the radio? They can see it.' And my dad had a two-word answer: 'Vin Scully.' He said they understand the game more. They understand the players and the history and the context," Garcetti said. "Vin Scully, you have taught us all baseball."

Scully plans to be there today for the Dodgers' home opener against the Arizona Diamondbacks. It will be his last home opener, despite the crowd's chants for him to continue on for one more year.

"I've done enough," he said. "I still have this year left again, God-willing, and maybe on the final day of my final broadcast, I'll somehow come up with the magic words that you deserve. As for now, I have only two magic words: thank you." ∎

VIN SCULLY'S 10 MOST MEMORABLE CALLS

By Tom Hoffarth | September 22, 2016

He called Don Larsen's 1956 World Series perfect game. He called Jack Nicklaus' march up the 18th fairway en route to a Masters victory.

But there are some calls in Vin Scully's career that are far more memorable when paired up with the events as they took place live.

While the Dodgers have conducted their own poll of his best calls of all time, here are 10 from his entire career that we believe are the most representative, most repeated, most impactful, and most inspirational:

No. 1: "In a year that has been so improbable, the impossible has happened."

Oct. 15, 1988, Kirk Gibson's game-winning homer in the bottom of the ninth in Game 1 of the World Series between the Dodgers and Oakland A's. Fortunately, he was on that call on a national TV basis for NBC. Gibson's entire at-bat is also described to perfection.

No. 2: "What a marvelous moment for baseball; what a marvelous moment for Atlanta and the state of Georgia; what a marvelous moment for the country and the world. A Black man is getting a standing ovation in the Deep South for breaking a record of an all-time baseball idol. And it is a great moment for all of us, and particularly for Henry Aaron."

April 8, 1974, calling Henry Aaron's 715th home run with the Dodgers in Atlanta at Fulton County Stadium.

After describing the home run, "Buckner goes back to the fence, it is gone!" Scully does not say another word until 1 minute, 10 seconds later when he says "What a marvelous moment."

No. 3: "Little roller up first, behind the bag, it gets through Buckner, here comes Knight and the Mets win it!"

Oct. 25, 1986 at Shea Stadium in Queens, New York, Game 6 of the World Series, capping a three-run rally by the Mets over the Boston Red Sox on Mookie Wilson's ground ball misplayed by Bill Buckner.

No. 4: "Two and two to Harvey Kuenn, one strike away, Sandy into his windup, here's the pitch ... swung on and missed, a perfect game!"

The final call of Sandy Koufax's perfect game against the Chicago Cubs on Sept. 9, 1965, on radio (no TV). The transcript of this entire ninth inning reads like a poem.

One of the most iconic plays in baseball history, Kirk Gibson's game-winning homer in the bottom of the ninth inning in Game 1 of the 1988 World Series stands out as the most memorable call of Vin Scully's illustrious career. (AP Images)

No. 5: **"If I'm to be honest with you and myself today, I have to ask ... why me? Why would a red-haired kid with a hole in his pants and his shirt tail hanging out playing stickball in the streets of New York wind up in Cooperstown?"**

From his four-minute speech upon his Hall of Fame induction in 1982 for the Ford C. Frick Award.

No. 6: **"If you have a sombrero, throw it to the sky!"**

Capping off the June 29, 1990 no-hitter by Fernando Valenzuela that ended with a double play grounder at Dodger Stadium. Scully starts the inning with the phrase: "It is the 29th of June, in case some day long from now Fernando is playing this back to his grandchildren."

No. 7: **"Bo Jackson says hello!"**

July 11, 1989, at the All-Star Game at Anaheim Stadium, as he's working the first inning for NBC with president Ronald Reagan in the booth. Bo Jackson leads the game off with a towering homer off Rick Reuschel.

No. 8: **"Montana ... looking ... looking .. throwing in the end zone ... Clark caught it! It's a madhouse at Candlestick with 51 seconds left. Dwight Clark is 6-4, he stands about 10 feet tall in this crowd's estimation."**

Jan. 10, 1982, NFC championship game on CBS between San Francisco and Dallas. The Catch.

Former Dodgers greats Steve Yeager, left, Fernando Valenzuela (Call No. 6) and Vin Scully before Game 2 of the 2017 World Series. (Los Angeles Daily News: Keith Birmingham)

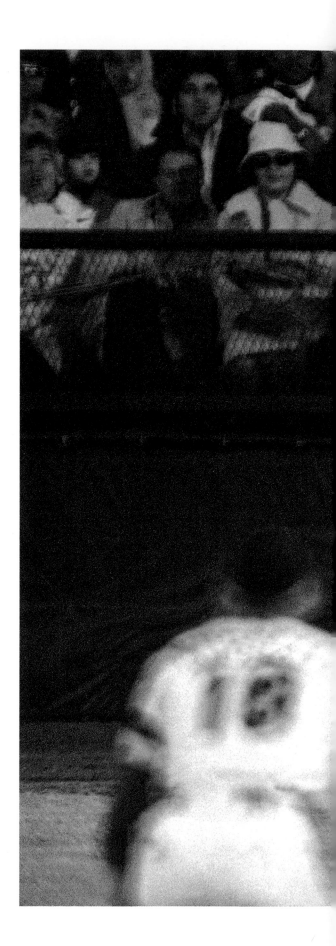

No. 9: **"And now, with the bases loaded, the infield is up, the outfield looks like a softball game, and the batter is R.J. Reynolds. ... Squeeze! And here comes the run! He squeezed it in!"**

The game is on Sept. 11, 1983 and has been called one of the greatest in Dodger Stadium history. The Dodgers' 7-6 win over the Atlanta Braves with a four-run ninth was decided when a little-known pinch hitter named R.J. Reynolds surprised everyone with a squeeze bunt to force in the winning run — actually, it was ruled a bunt single, eventually.

No. 10: **"The cathedral that is Yankee Stadium belongs to a Chapel."**

An ad-libbed line as he played himself in the movie "For Love of the Game" in 1999, in reference to Detroit Tigers pitcher Billy Chapel (Kevin Costner) throwing a perfect game in his final appearance.

Scully also said: "You get the feeling that Billy Chapel isn't pitching against left-handers, he isn't pitching against pinch hitters, he isn't pitching against the Yankees. He's pitching against time. He's pitching against the future, against age, and even when you think about his career, against ending. And tonight I think he might be able to use that aching old arm one more time to push the sun back up in the sky and give us one more day of summer." ■

One of the most memorable plays and calls in sports history, Hank Aaron eyes the flight of the ball after hitting his 715th career homer in a game against the Dodgers. Aaron broke Babe Ruth's record of 714 career home runs. Dodgers southpaw pitcher Al Downing, catcher Joe Ferguson and umpire David Davidson look on. (AP Images)

VIN SCULLY BY THE NUMBERS

By Tom Hoffarth | September 23, 2016

We'd never pegged Vin Scully as a numbers guy.

Asked recently to estimate how many baseball games he has called since breaking in with the Dodgers in 1950, the Hall of Fame broadcaster said: "Quite frankly, I have zero interest in knowing how many games I've done. It doesn't mean that much."

You could try to do the math and come up with … does more than 10,000 sound right?

Yet here we are trying to get our head around 67 seasons with the Dodgers, and 88 years, 10 months and three days old when he plans to do his final broadcast for the team Oct. 2 in San Francisco.

Here are other digits worth deciphering as to what is being accomplished here:

24,274: Days Scully has been with the team when he does his last game.

45.5: Percentage of years Scully has been involved as a broadcaster in Major League Baseball since the game's origins were established 147 years ago in 1869.

53: Percentage of years Scully has been involved as a broadcaster for the Dodgers with the franchise start date in Brooklyn 126 years ago in 1890.

33: Seasons Scully had been broadcasting Dodgers games before he was awarded the Ford Frick Award by the Baseball Hall of Fame in Cooperstown (inducted in 1982).

34: Seasons Scully has been broadcasting Dodgers games since his Hall of Fame induction. Does he deserve a second induction?

80: Age difference of Preacher Roe and Julio Urias, two pitchers whose games Scully has called in his career.

9: Different ownership groups under his time since 1950 — the first included Branch Rickey (who hired him), Walter O'Malley, James Lawrence Smith and James and Dearie Mulvey.

28: World Series calls on TV and radio (a broadcasting record).

6: World Series championships he has called for the Dodgers (1955, 1959, 1963, 1965, 1981 and 1988).

13: World Series Scully has called for the Dodgers.

21: No-hitters called — 14 by Dodgers pitchers (four by Sandy Koufax, two by Carl Erskine and one by Sal Maglie, Bill Singer, Fernando Valenzuela, Jerry Reuss, Kevin Gross, Ramon Martinez, Hideo Nomo and Clayton Kershaw). Six were by Dodgers opponents (Vern Bickford, Don Larsen, John Candelaria, Nolan Ryan, Dennis Martinez and Kent Mercker.) One was during a national NBC telecast (Jack Morris).

The breadth of time that Vin Scully has broadcasted and scope of baseball history that he's witnessed is unlike any other announcer. (Los Angeles Daily News: Keith Birmingham)

3: Perfect games called. By Larson (1955 World Series Game 5), Koufax (1965 vs. Chicago) and Martinez (1991 vs. the Dodgers). He was on an NBC assignment in 1988 when the Reds' Tom Browning threw a perfect game against the Dodgers.

9: Primary fellow Dodgers broadcasters Scully has worked with in either the TV or radio booth: Red Barber, Connie Desmond, Andre Baruch, Al Helfer and Jerry Doggett in Brooklyn, plus Ross Porter, Don Drysdale, Rick Monday and Charley Steiner in L.A. The Dodgers have also employed as broadcasters from 1950 to present: Al Downing, Jerry Reuss, Joe Davis, Orel Hershiser, Nomar Garciaparra, Eric Collins and Steve Lyons and Kevin Kennedy. The pay-service ON TV once had Geoff Witcher and Eddie Doucette call games with Downing (1980-84), A Dodgervision production had Doucette, Downing and Monday do games from 1985-87, Z Channel had Monday and Doucette work with Tony Hernandez, Monday and

Don Sutton ('88 and '89) and SportsChannel LA had Joel Meyers, Ron Cey and Duke Snider involved (1990-92). Since 1958, the Dodgers have also had 10 Spanish-language broadcasters, including Baseball Hall of Famer Jaime Jarrin (1959-to-present).

1: Ranking, in the 2005 Curt Smith book, "Voices of Summer: Ranking Baseball's 101 All-Time Best Announcers." In a grading process that gives 1-to-10 points in the categories of longevity, continuity, network presence, awards, language, popularity, persona, voice, knowledge and miscellany, Scully was the only one to score 100. Says a review from Booklist: "His top pick, Dodger announcer Vin Scully, may be beyond argument; everyone else is fair game." Mel Allen (99), Ernie Harwell (97), Jack Buck (96), Red Barber (95), Harry Caray and Bob Prince (94), Jack Brickhouse (93), Dizzy Dean and Lindsey Nelson (92) complete the top 10. ∎

'WHEN WE HELD OUR BREATH, YOU FILLED IN THE BLANKS'

Vin Scully Appreciation Night Turns Dodger Stadium into a Shrine

By J.P. Hoornstra | September 24, 2016

Forty cities and two counties declared Friday, September 23, as Vin Scully Day. It began like almost any other day at Dodger Stadium. The Dodgers stretched and played catch. The Colorado Rockies took batting practice. Continuing a recent tradition, some players visited the Vin Scully Press Box before the game to shake hands with the man himself.

"To kind of show respect to him, for what he's done for a long time," Dodgers pitcher Joe Blanton said. "He's one of the greatest announcers of all time. Just on a personal level, to be able to go up in his press box, shake his hand — I don't do a whole lot of stuff like that and it was a pretty cool little moment like that to have."

The game was scheduled to begin at 7:20 p.m. Pacific Time, but the first pitch was delayed by 27 minutes. In the meantime, a Vin Scully appreciation ceremony took over the field, turning a ballpark into a shrine — and turning Friday into more than just another stop on Scully's retirement tour.

Los Angeles mayor Eric Garcetti gave Scully a key to the city — a first in his three-plus years on the job, he said. Baseball commissioner Rob Manfred announced a $50,000 donation to the Jackie Robinson Foundation in Scully's name, and Dodgers manager Dave Roberts emerged from the dugout with an oversized check.

Kirk Gibson couldn't attend in person, but he wanted to pass along a pre-recorded message.

"It's an honor for me to have your voice attached to the soundtrack of my career," Gibson said, moments after it was revealed that fans voted Scully's 19-word description of Gibson's home run in Game 1 of the 1988 World Series as his greatest call ever.

Dodgers chairman Mark Walter announced that next year Scully would have a place among the team's list of retired numbers. As of Friday the team hadn't decided what will symbolize Scully, the first non-player to join the group.

One of the 10 Dodger players whose number is retired, Sandy Koufax, recounted a story about Scully.

"Before the World Series, Vin would go to church and pray — not for a win, but there would be only heroes in the World Series, no goats," Koufax said. "He didn't want anyone's future to be tarnished with the fact that they lost the World Series for their team."

Clayton Kershaw was the only current Dodger player sitting on the dais. He thanked Scully "on behalf of our team and the teams that have come before us."

"Thank you for painting a picture for us and for our families that we'll have for the rest of our lives," Kershaw said. "When we retire and we don't have this game anymore, we'll always have your voice. So thank you for that."

Vin Scully speaks with actor Kevin Costner during a ceremony honoring Scully at Dodger Stadium on Sept. 23, 2016. (Los Angeles Daily News: Keith Birmingham)

Actor Kevin Costner was the last guest speaker. He delivered a riveting speech that alternated between tongue-in-cheek humor ("you called my imaginary perfect game; nobody can ever take that away") and touching prose ("when we held our breath, you filled in the blanks").

Finally, Scully spoke. He had fought back tears when the emcee, Dodgers broadcaster Charley Steiner, introduced him on stage. He appeared fidgety as the distinguished speakers delivered one tribute after another.

Speaking to the sold-out crowd, Scully sounded right at home.

"When you roar, when you are thrilled, I'm 8 years old again," he said. "You truly have been the wind beneath my wings. I owe you everything." ■

LEAVING ON TOP

Scully Walks Out of Our Lives and Into His Own

By Mark Whicker | September 24, 2016

With five games to go in his 67th season, Vin Scully said, "Wow." With four games to go, he said, "Whoa."

He has seen Bobby Thomson's home run and Don Drysdale's shutout streak and then Orel Hershiser's. His amazement threshold is high.

Yet Scully has kept both feet in the broadcast booth until it all ends in San Francisco next Sunday, and his eyes look straight ahead and down at the only thing that matters.

He is going out like David Ortiz, deep inside the game, and unchallenged.

Yasiel Puig's throw made Scully gasp Wednesday. Chase Utley's behind-the-back throw from the prone position was the thrill on Thursday.

After each game this season, Scully has walked out with guards and between barricades as fans gather and beseech him for one more year, which is both unreasonable and natural.

As a performer Scully can handle the lovefest without squirming, but he'd prefer to hang around the dining room and trade stories with scouts, without the Secret Service. He finds peace on Sunday mornings, when he sits in the front row at chapel service, in the interview room near the clubhouse.

"They'll miss me for a year," he said, back in July. "They missed Harry Caray for a year, Jack Brickhouse, Jack Buck. Then they move on."

Probably not. But the intensity of the farewell is exactly right. He is the one shared experience in a city that speaks 224 languages, the only issue on which we all agree.

He saw Juan Marichal bludgeon Johnny Roseboro and he saw four Dodgers hit consecutive ninth-inning home runs, and he saw Rick Monday win a pennant with his bat and save an American flag.

He still has room for a "wow."

What makes Vin Vin?

The sad irony is that baseball clubs have learned nothing from Scully. They honor him and yet they keep hiring his antitheses.

He is rigidly non-partisan and, most nights, discusses opposing players more than Dodgers. Scully finds anecdotes that you've never heard before, even

Vin Scully's preparation and attention to detail are some of the many traits that made him a legend. (AP Images)

in the information age. When someone mentioned that he must have great researchers, Scully shook his head. He does it all himself, right to the finish line.

Nor is Scully interested in umpiring. He doesn't like the superimposed strike zones that networks use. "The umpire has a hard enough job as it is," he said.

Nor has Scully allowed decimal points to impede his enjoyment, and therefore ours. He will say a player is hitting "just over 300," or that a pitcher's ERA is "2.7." Joe Davis, whom the Dodgers hired last year to do road games in Scully's stead, recently declared that Fangraphs had decided Utley "is the 13th best baserunner in the game since 1950." What does that really mean? In Scully's booth, it would take up too much baseball to explain.

And it is Scully's booth. The solo method allows him to tell stories that he can finish next inning, if necessary. He leads us down his own roads.

As a fellow broadcaster recently said, "The (production) truck follows Vin. Everywhere else, the play-by-play man follows the truck."

Peer review

Marty Brennaman has done Cincinnati Reds' games since 1974. Scully once asked him if he ever took time off.

"I take off when the team has a day off," Brennaman said.

"Surely you're not laboring under the illusion that they can't play unless you're there," Scully replied.

"It was the best advice I ever got," Brennaman said in June, when the Reds came to Dodger Stadium.

He was planning to stay home during that trip. Then he realized that he wouldn't see Scully during the final season. He changed plans.

"He's the best storyteller that ever lived," Brennaman said. "He might see something that reminds him something that happened in Ebbets Field in 1953. And he does it in a conversational way that makes it seem like he's sitting across the table.

Vin Scully receives the key to the city from Los Angeles Mayor Eric Garcetti during a ceremony honoring Scully at Dodger Stadium. (Los Angeles Daily News: Hans Gutknecht)

Vin Scully and his wife Sandi take in a standing ovation during the ceremony celebrating Scully's career.
(Los Angeles Daily News: Hans Gutknecht)

"You have to have a voice that wears well. He doesn't sound any different than 40 years ago. But beyond all that, he's humble as hell, the most approachable, nicest man you ever met."

Scully's voice is a natural resource that can't really be explained. Voices get fainter and scratchier when they age. His baritone is somehow richer.

Adele Cabot, a renowned L.A. voice coach, said it could just be spiritual, that Scully's zest for baseball brings out the technique and the proper breathing. She may be onto something. On the day Don Drysdale died in 1993, Scully was subdued and mournful, not himself at all, as he talked from Montreal.

"I don't know how he does it," said Eric Nadel, the Texas Rangers' play-by-play man. "I do six innings. He does nine. I drink water for my voice. Pat Hughes (Cubs) drinks tea during the game. Some of us gargle. He started doing this the year I was born.

"For years I'd listen to him in preseason. I might be hiking, might be in a hot tub, but I'd always have a pen next to me. The way he describes shadows on the field, body language of a pitcher, nobody comes close to that."

Most announcers get fired, of course. Some get promoted. Few get to decide how it ends.

"He hasn't had to make those concessions," Nadel said. "You listen and you're instantly in the presence of somebody who's happy to be where he is.

"The smile in his voice stands out."

Unplugged

Scully is the most publicly private man you'll meet. There are no authorized biographies of Scully, and he has spent all these 67 years — 70, if you add the accumulated time he's spent waiting for the Dodger Stadium elevator — with a tight wrap on his non-baseball opinions.

Lately he has unplugged himself a bit.

One night he devoted a couple of innings to contradictory facts. "Do you know how long the Hundred Years' War lasted? One hundred sixteen years," he said. "Okay, just one more…"

He abjectly refused to try the name of Cubs reliever Rob Zastryzny, which brought back the hilarity of the day he talked of the broadcaster's nightmare: "A rundown involving Chin-feng Chen and Chin-hui Tsao."

You can tell his annoyance with the modern game when he says, "We've had 11 relief pitchers in this little gem."

You can hear the lament over a player's obstinance when he says of Arizona's struggling Shelby Miller, "I wonder how many kids have had their careers ruined by that Frank Sinatra song, 'I did it my way.'"

Several years ago, off the air, he noted the swollen salaries, and the sensory assault by stadium loudspeakers, and he made a prediction.

"Before I retire I'm going to see two things," he said. "One will be a player who is making so much money that he hires someone to play the game for him.

"The other will happen before a game. A human sacrifice."

Instead he walks out of our lives and into his own, having given us a year's warning to gather all the DVRs and tape recordings, all equipped with a smile in his voice. ∎

GUIDING SPIRIT

Vin Scully Wants to be Known as 'A Man Who Lived Up to His Own Beliefs'

By Tom Hoffarth | September 25, 2016

It was another question that had to do with his recollections of Kirk Gibson's Hollywood-like feat in Game 1 of the 1988 World Series.

Vin Scully admitted it was the "most theatrical home run" he had ever called. "Also the most surprising," he added.

But then the Dodgers Hall of Fame broadcaster had one more confession to make to the 50-some members of the media who had crowded into the interview room on the bottom floor of Dodger Stadium on Saturday afternoon.

"I do remember — it's wasn't a prayer exactly — but I remember saying, 'Dear God, let him hit the ball. Don't let him strike out. He's had such a big year and meant so much, and this is the national stage. A good fly ball would be great.'

"And then when he hit the home run … I had a lot of trouble sitting down because of so much nervous energy. But that gave me a moment — where it came from, God must have sent it to me … 'In the year of the improbable …'"

Al Michaels wonders if we believe in miracles. But it's not impossible that this was another act of divine intervention, somehow connected to Scully's belief in a higher power.

God only knows.

Mass Appeal

There's a Scully-narrated commercial that SportsNet LA will occasionally air, his words overlaid on video of him gazing out of his press box booth and strolling across the outfield grass.

"When I walk inside the walls of cathedral-like Dodger Stadium, I hear the echoes of stories that brought crowds to their feet … and let's face it, even tears to the eyes of the faithful," he says.

In truth, Dodger Stadium does become very cathedral-like, albeit on a much smaller scale, every Sunday morning before a home game.

Inside that very same room where Scully told story after story during a final group Q-and-A session on Saturday, he will join some Dodger players, coaches and stadium employees in attending a Catholic Mass just hours before he goes to the broadcast booth for the final time in his 67-season career.

A white altar cloth will cover the long table where Dave Roberts holds his postgame press conference, and a visiting priest will be invited by Catholic Athletes for Christ organization to celebrate.

Scully takes his seat in the front row, often next to his wife, Sandi. A chair to his right is left vacant and a Dodgers jacket is draped across the back. It is there to remember Billy DeLury, the former team traveling

Vin Scully talks with his granddaughters before a game against the Diamondbacks on Sept. 23, 2015. Scully was given a Guinness World Records certificate for the longest career as a sports broadcaster for a single team, and the team honored him with a bobble head for all fans in attendance. (AP Images)

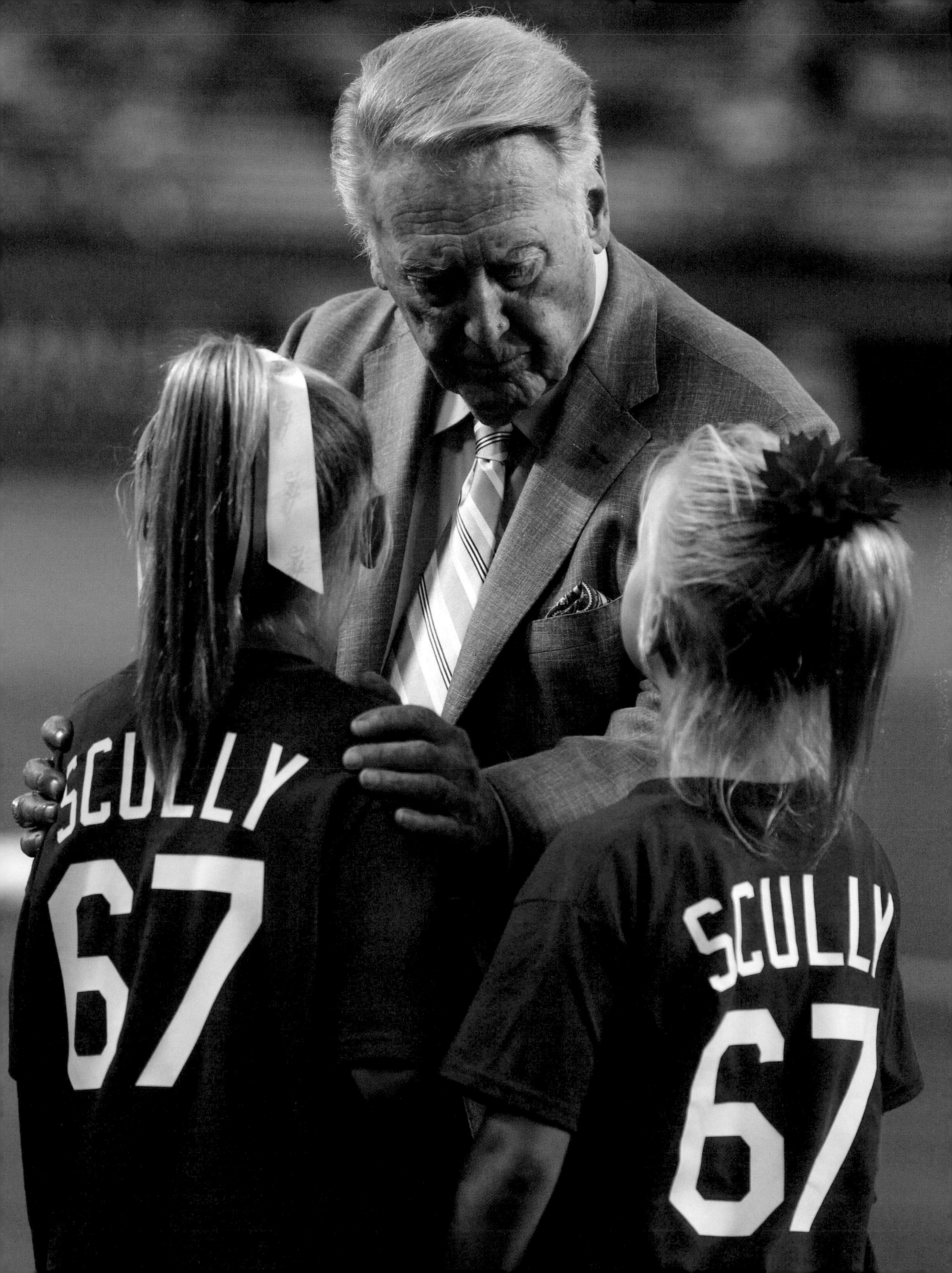
SCULLY
67
SCULLY
67

secretary who traveled from Brooklyn to Los Angeles with Scully in 1958 and died at age 81 just before the 2015 season began.

And when it comes to the Bible readings, Scully will often volunteer to act as the lector.

Really, if you want to make God smile, let him hear Scully read the Book of Wisdom. Chapter and verse.

A story about Scully in the October edition of the Catholic Digest asked him if he, because of his religious beliefs, felt he already had one foot in heaven.

"I don't feel like I have one foot in heaven," he said, "but I think I can see it from here, especially at Mass."

When searching for all the possible reasons why Scully is so genuinely humble, gracious and grateful, he will circle back to his upbringing in an Irish Catholic home, attending Catholic schools where the nuns tried to shake him of his habit of writing with his left hand ("they thought it would make me stutter," he said), going to the Jesuit-taught all-boys Fordham Prep School in the Bronx and then graduating from Fordham University in the Bronx.

"God has been incredibly kind to allow me to be in the position to watch and to broadcast all these somewhat monumental events," Scully, who regularly attends Mass at St. Jude the Apostle Church in Westlake Village, said earlier this week. "I'm really filled with thanksgiving and the fact that I've been given such a chance to view. But none of those are my achievements; I just happened to be there. … I know some people won't understand it, but I think it has been God's generosity to put me in these places and let me enjoy it."

He has also said recently: "All I know is that I'm profoundly humbled and grateful to the Lord for the gift of being able to cover baseball for practically my whole adult life. When the time comes to sign off for good, I'll look back with joy."

A Humble Servant

The members of the media wouldn't leave Saturday until told they had to. Scully told story after story, and the half-hour allotted time started to go past 45 minutes, and then closer to an hour.

How did he feel on Friday night after his appreciation ceremony? "You've heard about being on Mt. Olympus? I was five feet above that," Scully admitted.

How do you think you'll feel on the Monday after your last game? "Maybe I'll take my watch off and just put it in the drawer," he guessed.

And then, as the Dodgers' PR people decided it was time for Scully to go back to the Vin Scully Press Box and finish preparing for Saturday night's game, everyone in the room gave him a standing ovation.

Scully blushed. Again.

Orel Hershiser, the former Dodgers pitcher and World Series hero who was known for his religious conviction giving him strength during the rough-and-tumble 1988 playoff run, has said in SportsNet L.A. commercial spots: "He will remind us about who we are supposed to be, still. Because that's what he taught us … how to be gentlemen. How to have integrity. He taught us how to hold this place up in the highest esteem and live your life accordingly. That's what I'll miss, that example."

It reminds us of a story he told about himself on the air earlier this season — a moment during his first year, 1950, when leaving Ebbets Field on a rainy Saturday afternoon after the Dodgers played the St. Louis Cardinals.

"There were hundreds of kids running toward me with paper wanting an autograph," he said. "I was starting to write my name on a piece the paper, and way in the back, a kid hollered, 'Who is it?' And the kid in the front said, 'Vin … uh …. Scully?' And the

Vin Scully served as an example of integrity and conviction throughout his nearly seven decades as a broadcaster. (Los Angeles Daily News: John McCoy)

kid in the back yelled, 'He's nobody!' And the 500 kids walked away."

Scully laughed, surmising that since he was wearing a raincoat and hat and had red hair, the kids must have thought he was Red Schoendienst.

"I never forgot that," said Scully. "And you know what? He was right. Who the heck was I?"

Today, Scully says he identifies as someone who wants to be remembered not as a sportscaster, but "the very normal guy that I am. I just want to be remembered as a good man, an honest man, and one who lived up to his own beliefs."

We believe that's what will happen. The answer to our prayers, as well as his. ∎

BIGGER THAN THE GAME ITSELF

For Generations of Dodgers Fans, Vin Scully is The Tie that Binds

By Ryan Kartje | September 26, 2016

The voice is unmistakable — a warm, velvety tenor, so rich in tone, so rhythmic in its pace — like the croon of a classic standard. In Los Angeles, a city of constant reinvention, where transience is a way of life, the voice has endured for nearly seven decades. "The soundtrack of summer," it is so warmly labeled.

But to those who have faithfully tuned in over the years, the voice transcends the images that title conjures — of sun-drenched afternoons in the shade of palm trees, of Dodger dogs and baseball in Chavez Ravine. To many here, the voice is bigger than the game itself.

Years after the transistor radio became a relic, replaced by MLB TV and live updates on iPhone screens, the voice remains a time machine. Close your eyes, and you'll practically smell the fresh-cut grass in center field, taste the fresh-squeezed lemonade, hear the crack of the bat and crackle of the radio dial. To listen in is to be transported across generations.

"Pull up a chair," Vin Scully asks at the top of his Dodgers broadcast, inviting you in once again as his personal guest. Over 67 years, he has become America's most trusted storyteller, sports or otherwise, his tales so artfully intertwined with balls and strikes that it feels as if Scully pulls the game's strings himself.

He is baseball's omniscient narrator, after all, the voice behind Kirk Gibson's famous hobbled walk-off home run in the 1988 World Series — "In a year that has been so improbable, the impossible has happened!" — and baseball's most infamous World Series gaffe — "It gets through Buckner!" Scully has been a part of each of the Dodgers' six World Series titles and all four of Sandy Koufax's no-hitters. His career stretches from Jackie Robinson's prime in Brooklyn to Clayton Kershaw's in L.A. — an astounding span of almost 10,000 games.

"There's no way to separate him from the team's identity," says Steve Kaminsky, 71, of South Pasadena, a New York transplant and listener for more than 60 years. "Vinny has always been there."

Scully broadcast his final Dodgers home game Sunday. On October 2, the magical 67-year run of broadcasting's most beloved voice will come to an end in San Francisco. Just shy of his 88th birthday, Scully will bid the baseball world adieu, and fans far and wide, young and old, will collectively mourn. In Los Angeles, the most loyal of Scully's listeners liken his departure to losing a family member.

To say goodbye, they say, feels like ending a decades-long conversation, as if, in all those years of stitching together baseball soliloquy alone in his

Generations of Dodgers fans grew up on the voice of Vin Scully and had a hard time saying goodbye, both when his announcing days concluded and when he passed away. (AP Images)

Dodger Stadium booth, his stories and his magic are not meant for the millions on freeways and in their living rooms, but for you, wherever you may be.

"I've always felt that I was talking to one person," Scully once said. "But I've never envisioned who that one person is."

From Brooklyn to Beverly Hills

Larry King was 16 years old when he heard the voice from the bulky set of his transistor radio. Even then, he remembers being drawn in. From the living room of his current home in Beverly Hills, he's transported back to that afternoon in 1950 — his family's tiny Brooklyn apartment, the crackle of the radio, and Dodgers announcer Red Barber with the microphone, handing off to a "young man out of Fordham" for the first time.

"Here," Barber announced, "is the voice of Vin Scully."

As a child, King's only reference to his beloved Dodgers was Barber's voice. His father died suddenly of a heart attack in June 1943 when he was just 9. And in the years that followed, King's family was the poorest on his block. Baseball tickets were an uncommon luxury, so he dreamed of the crisp white lines and fresh green grass of Ebbets Field.

The radio had been a Hanukkah present from his mother, soon after his father's death, and King often lugged the 40-pound set around on his shoulders, hanging on Barber's every word, imitating his voice to strangers.

It was in this imaginative world that Scully flourished. He described scenes in detailed brushstrokes, paying special care to nuance — the tug of a pitcher's collar or sweat wiped from a batter's forehead. In 1953, he called a World Series at just 25 years old, and the next season, took over full-time as voice of the Dodgers. Like his predecessor, Scully was a natural storyteller, and in the transistor radio, he found his perfect medium — an open stoop, on which

he could sling his press-box poetry.

The Dodgers won their first World Series in 1955, and as left-hander Johnny Podres induced the final ground out of a Game 7 shutout, King burst through the door of his apartment. The sound of Scully's voice poured into the street with him, from transistors across the neighborhood.

In that moment, Scully's voice seemed to ring down from on high: "Ladies and gentlemen," he declared, "the Brooklyn Dodgers are the champions of the world." The call set off a celebration; the entire borough had been waiting for him to confirm. When the Dodgers moved west in 1958, Angelenos would feel the same, distrusting their own eyes, until Vin had said it was true.

"Baseball announcers were a part of you then," King remembers. "They were your lifeblood. There aren't many like that anymore."

As the transistor's popularity diminished, the gravitas of baseball's finest wordsmiths did, as well. Memories of the greats — Barber, Mel Allen, Russ Hodges, Ernie Harwell, each once as famous as the game they announced — have faded. Even King, known for his iconic radio personality, has been forced to adapt. His voice is now heard almost exclusively on Hulu, streamed for millions over the Internet.

"The world really has changed," he says.

Down the hallway, a collection of sports relics and personal keepsakes, all juxtaposed together, line the halls of a room that's as much museum as it is family trophy room. Cardboard cutouts from his sons' little league baseball teams rest near a pair of Muhammad Ali's boxing gloves. Dozens of autographed balls and gloves and shoes are scattered between photos of King with U.S. presidents and celebrities.

Near the door, an original painting of Ebbets Field hangs on its own, and as he offers a rare tour, King stops in front of it. In the first row, behind home plate, there he is, with his Dodger hat and dark-rimmed glasses,

Ebbets Field, the home of the Brooklyn Dodgers and site of the start of Vin Scully's amazing career. (AP Images)

painted into the Brooklyn crowd, frozen in time.

In this room, the past breathes with life, but outside, King is constantly reminded of how much time has changed what he once knew. Just to listen to Scully, he switches his television from DirecTV to a second provider, Time Warner, which, due to a TV dispute, he had to buy to even watch the Dodgers. Sometimes, he yearns again for the simplicity of his transistor radio.

King wonders about his youngest sons, Chance and Cannon, and how they'll remember Scully or the other greats, if they'll remember at all. He calls Cannon into the room. "What does Vin mean to you?" he asks.

"You hear his voice, and I don't know," Cannon says, "there's just nothing like it."

It's true — Scully is the last vestige of a bygone time, and King wonders aloud what exactly that will mean for those who never knew that transistor era, apart from Scully and the nostalgia his voice conjures. But here again, with his impeccable timing, Scully sweeps him off his feet, launching into a story about Frank Sinatra's song "My Way."

"As Sinatra said, 'There's a lot to said for longevity,'" King recites, as Scully hums along in the background. "You can't fool people for 67 years."

But after all that time, after the world has changed again and again, how will baseball remember its most iconic announcer and the era he leaves behind? Can a voice so constant ever truly fade? A beat passes, and Scully's timeless cadence fills the room again.

"Ah, that voice," King says, trailing off. For the moment, it's all that seems to matter.

Bedtime Stories

It's 9:30 p.m., well past his bedtime, but 8-year-old Jonathan Lobel is still awake, with headphones on, as his mother, Michelle, opens the bedroom door. The jig is up. "It's the bottom of the eighth!" he begs.

This time, she'll let it slide. Only a couple more days of summer remain, after all, and in this final season of Scully, what could a few more minutes hurt?

Jonathan is almost certainly the only second-grader in Los Angeles spellbound nightly by Vin's voice on the transistor radio. Every night, in a room filled with autographed baseballs and bobbleheads, he sets his small, silver radio on his nightstand, slips on black headphones, and closes his eyes, as Scully's words paint the scene.

The arrangement began as a compromise. Jonathan's bedtime on school nights meant missing most of the Dodgers broadcast on TV. But as his son grew older, Jonathan's father worried television was distracting from what, he remembered, made baseball so magical. So Josh Lobel, a hedge fund manager in Beverly Hills, bought his son a transistor radio.

"We live in such a visual culture, and we've lost so much magic in the story," Josh says. "I wanted him to see it all, the way I did listening to Vin."

Perhaps it sounds contradictory — that only on the radio can we truly "see" — but consider this: Since making their deal, Jonathan's knowledge of the team has become encyclopedic. On the day backup catcher A.J. Ellis is traded to the Phillies, he conjures statistics out of thin air to analyze the fallout. For fun, earlier this season, Jonathan and his father created a computer spreadsheet to predict the Dodgers' final record. His estimate called for the Dodgers to win the NL West by six games; as of this weekend, they lead the Giants by that exact margin.

There were other signs of Scully's influence: Players nearly three times Jonathan's age were suddenly "youngsters." One night, he announced to the family that a home run was "hit from here to Utica!"

"We realized he was being raised by an 87-year-old for two hours a night," Josh says.

His father understands their deal can't possibly last. Even Jonathan admits he prefers to watch on TV. But Josh will settle for knowing that, however briefly, he

Fans listen to Vin Scully during Vin Scully Appreciation Day on Sept. 23, 2016. (AP Images)

and his son shared in the magic of Scully on the radio, like he and his father once did.

"I was wondering," Jonathan asks, "if the Dodgers won the World Series, do you think he would stay?"

He wants to believe it's possible — or, at least, that his replacement might actually fill his shoes — but as the voices of Lobel children fill the living room, drowning out the broadcast, there's no time to dwell on such a dream. It's well past Jonathan's bedtime again.

And upstairs, on the nightstand in his room, a voice beckons from the transistor.

A Second Dad

For more than seven hours, Dee Audette sat in a chair at a Hollywood tattoo parlor as an ink portrait of the 80-year-old man she'd come to love, but had never met, began to take shape on her right forearm.

Etched from wrist to elbow was his toothy smile, his perfectly coiffed red hair, and his impeccable suit, shaded black and outfitted with a striped tie. As the needle colored in the contours of his face and the wrinkles in his forehead, Audette only grew more confident. For Vin Scully, a tattoo seemed like the least she could do.

Audette grew up in East L.A., in a small house on Morrow Place, with seven brothers and sisters, too strapped to afford baseball tickets for a family of 10. So every night, they gathered in the living room to watch the Dodgers, and her father, Mike, would turn the television on mute and the radio on high. Together, they reveled in that night's stories, while she watched from her father's lap.

Over the years, father and daughter grew close. The Dodgers and Vin's velvety voice on the radio had been the source of their bond.

"I always thought of Vin as another dad," she says. "He was always there."

When her father died in 2001, the team and Scully became Audette's sole escape. She bought season tickets and started traveling to the park for nearly every game, like she always promised she would. She began collecting every keepsake she could and stashing it at home.

On opening day of the 2010 season, Scully's 60th year as the team's announcer, Audette went to Chavez Ravine determined to finally meet the man whose image she had tattooed on her arm.

As Scully came into view, Audette's heart raced. He introduced himself, before the sight of his ink-drawn likeness, smiling up from a strange woman's forearm turned him a bright shade of red.

"Why would you do that for me?" Scully asked her.

"Why would you give up 60 years for us Dodger fans?" she echoed back.

He invited her into the press box, and they talked baseball for the better part of an hour. He was just as she'd always envisioned — humble, kind, unflinchingly polite. By the end of their conversation, she was sitting on Scully's lap, just as she'd sat on her father's years ago. Tears welled up in her eyes, as he signed his name below the tattoo. She drove to Hollywood right away, to have it outlined in ink.

Audette, now nearing 50, admits she has not yet come to terms with the end. After news spread recently that Scully wouldn't continue through the playoffs, her husband, Kevin, came home to Audette balled up, in tears. "It's finally hitting me," she told him.

To Kevin, it was no surprise. Before he proposed, Audette warned that the Dodgers would always come first. He now drives a Dodger blue car, and the walls of their living room are lined with Dodgers memorabilia.

But all of it is secondary to the voice of her childhood, the man smiling up every day from her forearm.

"Without him," she says, "I can't even imagine. How will things even go on?"

The Dodgers tip their hats towards Vin Scully, who called his last Dodger home game of his 67-year career on Sept. 25, 2016. (AP Images)

Easing a Difficult Life

It was 31 years ago, aboard a cruise bound for the Mexican Riviera, that Colleen Owen had a serendipitous encounter with Vin Scully in the ship's gift shop.

Since her mother shook Jackie Robinson's hand, one morning in 1949, the Owens had been marked for Dodgers fandom. After dinner, the family often gathered in their usual spots around the bulky wooden console in the living room to watch the Dodgers. Scully's stories, night after night, were their soundtrack.

To her brother, especially, Scully was a hero. As a boy, Tom Owen dreamed of being a baseball announcer. He would ride his Stingray bike up and down the streets of their idyllic Simi Valley neighborhood, copying Scully's calls with a transistor radio held to one ear. With his bright red hair, family and friends called him "Little Vinny." The nickname stuck for years.

So when Colleen, the gift shop's manager, worked up the courage to approach Scully that day, she told him about Tom. The next morning, she woke to an envelope under her door. Inside was an 8×10 glossy autographed photo of Scully, along with a note, written on the back of his gift shop receipt.

"Hi Tom," it read, in loopy cursive. "Best wishes to a 'little Vinnie' — Vin Scully"

Six weeks before his final broadcast, Tom and Colleen (now Colleen Ortoli) sit at a table at the ESPN Zone in Anaheim as the Dodgers play on a nearby television, and the note to "Little Vinnie" sits on the table between them. All these years later, he has kept it close. Tom still feels an uncanny bond with the man who signed it.

Tom lives in Moorpark; Colleen is in Laguna Niguel. It has been a while since they've seen each other. But Scully's voice, humming along in the background, has a way of taking you back, and Tom, with his 1988 Kirk Gibson jersey slipped over a blue polo, is feeling nostalgic, reminiscing of nights in front of that 24-inch RCA, when he'd sit so close his mother worried he'd go blind.

"I had a one-track mind," he says, laughing. "It was the Dodgers and Vin Scully, all day."

If only life were as simple as it was then, as Scully's voice often makes it feel.

Since 2001, when multiple sclerosis first rendered his wife, Cathy, medically disabled, that voice has been Tom's lifeline. As her strength deteriorated and the weight of his own life overwhelmed him, Tom would sit in his recliner until well past midnight, just to hear Scully and let the world melt away for a while.

Cathy is not yet confined to a wheelchair, but close. The left side of her body often goes numb, and her vision comes and goes. Most nights, she's too tired to travel. So when Tom returns from his job at Sunbelt Rentals, he takes care of the housework, the laundry, and anything else Cathy might need, waiting until late into the night before he flips on the Dodgers replay.

All of it has taken its toll on Tom. He chokes up, thinking about what they've been through. At times, he says, he has struggled to cope.

"His life has not been easy," Colleen says, her eyes welling up.

During Scully's 67 years on the air, tragedy has been a constant visitor. In 1972, his first wife, Joan, overdosed on prescribed medication one night and never woke up. His booth partner, Don Drysdale, suffered a heart attack in 1993 and died suddenly in his hotel room. A year later, his eldest son, Michael, died in a helicopter crash while investigating the damage of the Northridge earthquake.

And yet, few ever sensed his heartbreak. Scully's voice never faltered. Tom wondered, sometimes, how he could possibly carry on through such darkness, but right on cue his voice fills the room. Tom wipes his eyes.

"Vin, he knows — he's always known — it's not about him," Tom says. "He's not living for just himself."

And of the many lessons he has learned from Scully over the years, culled from afternoons in the backyard or late nights in his Moorpark living room, this is the one he holds closest, as Scully's final season comes to a close.

Tom has tried not to think what life will be like without him. But as Scully would certainly tell him, there is plenty to be joyful about. The Dodgers are bound for the postseason. Cathy recently found an office job as a once-a-week sub that she loves. And soon, they will celebrate their 25th wedding anniversary.

"I just wish he would've met Vin," his sister says, packing away that note from three decades ago.

But in many ways, he already had. For Little Vinnie, Vin had been there all along.

Tie That Binds

Near the doorway of Gil Cedillo's office on the fourth floor of City Hall hangs a charcoal drawing of a bridge near the Boyle Heights home where he grew up. Since his election as city councilman, it has hung there as a metaphor. "Bridges bring people together," he explains.

The neighborhood around 1st and Evergreen was a tapestry of cultures in those days — a Jewish temple, a Chinese corner store, housing projects with mostly African-American families — and yet, for all their differences, there was one thing that brought the community together most. In the summer months, all you had to do was shut up and listen to understand, as Vin Scully's voice rang out from radios up and down the street.

"The Dodgers were affordable," says Cedillo, whose district includes Dodger Stadium. "They were working class. They were our team."

And Vin, by extension, was their voice. It's a wonder now: To look back on an era of such social unrest and see a white man, with that saccharine tenor and shock of red hair, bridge such a gap, speaking to all races, all classes, reaching them through the same microphone. Scully could quote from 19th-century Italian opera, and yet, still speak to the common man through his stories. In a city spread across 503 square miles, his voice was perpetually central.

"He was a bridge to our common history," Cedillo says. "We all felt like we knew him, like he was ours alone."

Last year, after turning it down time and again, Scully finally agreed to let the Dodgers dedicate the street outside Chavez Ravine in his honor. So the team called the local councilman, Cedillo, who cut a year-long process down to "a few months." Bureaucracy, it seems, has nothing on Vin.

The night before the dedication, Cedillo couldn't sleep. So he turned on a few of Scully's most famous calls for inspiration. Instantly, he was transported back to the transistor radio in his parents' kitchen; to chocolate malts in the cheap seats; to the inner rungs of Dodger Stadium and the back route only his father seemed to know. Even now, Scully had been a bridge back home, like the charcoal drawing in his office.

The next day, he stood next to Scully himself, holding up a sign for Vin Scully Avenue, the stadium he loved in the background. It felt like a dream. He snapped a photo with Scully to commemorate the occasion.

His speech? It came and went: "We all told the same story," Cedillo says, "of Vin and his voice on our transistor radios."

Final Curtain

At his most magical, in those rarest of times when even America's finest broadcaster and his melodic prose could not capture the tenor of the scene before him, Vin Scully would step away from the microphone and let the roar of the crowd wash over it all, beckoning us into the moment and its euphoria — the thump, thump, thump of fireworks over Hank Aaron's record home trot or the din of an organ's song as Kirk Gibson rounded the bases in '88.

For 30 seconds, for a minute, for longer — you were there, next to the man himself, basking in the scene he so eloquently set, until, at just the right moment, his voice filled the empty space again.

Soon, the curtain will fall on his 67th and final season, and that voice, the one that spoke to generations through their transistor radios, that so elegantly captured the soul of the game and the tone of sprawling Southern California, will welcome us in for one last conversation between friends.

And when the time is right, Vin Scully will pull up a chair and the baseball world will rise to its feet, as the weight of the moment and the roar of the crowd sweeps him away one final time. ∎

ENOUGH FOR A LIFETIME

The Voice of Dodger Baseball Bids Farewell in Final Broadcast

By Tom Hoffarth | October 2, 2016

I pulled up a chair — a beat-up old beach chair that should have fallen apart years ago.

I planted it in the sand a few yards from the waves and turned up the transistor radio.

Vin Scully opened the final Dodgers-Giants game of the 2016 season, and the last of his 67-year broadcasting career, with the usual pleasantries, and the words washed over us.

The 88-year-old Hall of Fame broadcaster established the ground rules: There was "a lot at stake for San Francisco," needing to win and get into that last National League playoff spot. The Dodgers just needed to stay healthy before starting the playoffs.

And there was "kind of an angry sky (earlier) but it's softened up a bit. … The sky has punctures in it with a little bit of blue overhead."

My eyes were closed and saw everything.

I pulled up a chair   the driver's seat of my car.

I drove to run some errands and listened to Scully keep calling things on the dashboard radio as the third inning started, the Giants already out to a 5-0 lead. As Scully went along for the ride, he wished Maury Wills a happy 84th birthday and told us that, for the Giants, "this is turning into a lovely day."

I pulled up a chair — the wooden Adirondack with the nice cushion.

In the backyard for a few minutes of rest after some yard work. With the transistor radio, we heard Willie Mays join Scully in the booth, and those in the stands were asked to honor him once more.

I pulled up a chair — a bar stool.

The patio grill was fired up for a package of foot-long Dodger Dogs. Scully said he hoped he "wasn't interrupting too much" of the game with all the things going on around him. He even admitted in the bottom of the sixth that while he was "jabbering away so much with all the stuff that's been going on … I forgot — I'm supposedly doing play-by-play for the entire game on radio. My apologies for those of you who are wondering what's going on here. It has been a retirement party, and it's been marvelous."

No need for a mea culpa.

I pulled up a chair — the living-room recliner.

During the seventh-inning stretch, Scully's version of "Take Me Out to the Ballgame" couldn't drown out a well-intentioned effort by Giants broadcaster Mike Krukow.

Eventually, the top of the ninth arrived, with the Giants cruising to a 7-1 victory and entry into the playoffs, and Scully captured the moment starting with a line that "I've been holding onto most of the year: 'Don't be sad that it's over, smile because

While Dodgers fans claimed Vin Scully as their own, appreciation for his greatness was expressed from fans all over the country during his last season broadcasting. (AP Images)

it happened.' And that's really how I feel about this remarkable opportunity that I was given and allowed to keep all these years."

Then came: "There's another line a great sportswriter wrote back in the '20s, A.J. Liebling: 'The world isn't going backward if you can just stay young enough to remember what it was like when you were really young.' How about that?"

Even through the watering eyes, we could see Scully prepare us for the inevitable.

Rob Segedin flied out to end it, and Scully reported all the important numbers, then admitted: "I have said enough for a lifetime, and for the last time, I wish you all a very pleasant good afternoon."

Except, it wasn't the last time.

After a video where Scully narrated some thoughts, he was back on the TV screen to leave us with this Irish poem:

"May God give your every storm, a rainbow; for every tear, a smile; for every care, a promise and a blessing in each trial. For every problem life seems, a faithful friend to share; for every sigh, a sweet song and an answer for each prayer.

"You and I have been friends for a long time. … I'll miss our time together more than I can say. But you know what? There will be a new day. And, eventually, a new year. And when the upcoming winter gives way to spring, rest assured it once again will be time for Dodger baseball. So this is Vin Scully, wishing you a very pleasant good afternoon, wherever you may be."

The cameras then pointed to the flags whipping on the roof of AT&T Park — showing the Dodgers' banner one rung above the Giants' — and the brisk San Francisco winds into the microphone sounded as if the heavens were giving Scully a thunderous ovation.

I pulled up a chair — not even sure which one at that point — sunk down, and had a good cry. ∎

In the weeks after his retirement, Vin Scully waves to the Dodger Stadium crowd during Game 5 of the 2016 NLCS. (Los Angeles Daily News: Hans Gutknecht)

SPORTS PERSON OF THE YEAR

2016 Belonged to Vin Scully

By Tom Hoffarth | December 30, 2016

In early October, St. John's Episcopal Church in Corona updated the "welcome" message on its street corner marquee. In addition to reminding worshipers about the times for the Sunday services, the clip-on letters spelled out a reminder:

"Be Like Vin Scully … Notice And Praise The Good In Everyone."

It was as if God just dropped the mic. There may not be another perfect thing to say, write or preach about our choice for the 2016 Southern California News Group Sports Person of the Year.

It was a year so improbable for nominees very well deserving of our annual recognition for the person, place or things that made the most news, good or bad, in our circulation area.

Stan Kroenke pulls off a move that brings the Rams back to L.A. Kobe Bryant's final NBA season capped by a 60-point performance. Mike Trout's second AL MVP season. Clay Helton's USC football team going from 1-3 to a Rose Bowl berth with quarterback Sam Darnold. LonzoBall's dynamic transition from Chino Hills High to UCLA. The Sparks' WNBA title sparked by Nneka Ogwumike. The return of California Chrome.

And now, did the impossible just happen — Scully, who turned 89 just after last Thanksgiving, has also dropped the mic?

He gave Los Angeles ample warning that his 67th Dodgers' season would "realistically" be it for him. Those of us with separation anxiety or fears of abandonment thought he could change his mind once the season began.

From the moment he appeared before an adoring crowd as part of the team's Fan Fest in January at Dodger Stadium, to having the stadium's address changed because of the street leading into was named for Scully, through his final memorable call in the Dodgers' final home game on Charlie Culberson's walk-off homer, Scully took more selfies and shook more hands — and perhaps granted more wishes — than Santa Claus.

So many well-wishers would come up to the broadcast booth in the course of the season that a security guard had to make sure you were on the list. A Scully appreciation night in late September, with a memorable speech delivered by Kevin Costner, will be forever kept on the DVR.

President Barack Obama presents the Presidential Medal of Freedom to Vin Scully in the East Room of the White House in Washington, D.C. on Nov. 22, 2016. (AP Images)

'Vin and Willie Were Holding Hands'

During Scully's final broadcast in San Francisco as the Dodgers ended the regular season on Sunday, Oct. 2, the long-time rival Giants unveiled a plaque in the AT&T Stadium press box to commemorate the site of his final call after more than 9,000-plus games.

Willie Mays, whom Scully said was the best player he ever saw as a broadcaster, was part of the ceremony. Knowing that Mays was all but blind these days at age 85, Scully gently took Mays' hands, led him over to the plaque on the wall, and ran Mays' fingers across the raised letters as he read them aloud.

Rob Menschel was with Scully in the press box that weekend as part of the production crew. The special moment he saw came the day before, on Saturday, when Mays met with Scully before that game. Menschel was shooting video.

"When I looked in my camera viewfinder, I noticed something that was truly beautiful: Vin and Willie were holding hands," said Menschel. "I focused on their hands. They continued their conversation for another five minutes so Vin could return to his game preparation.

"In a 10-day span that was filled with highly emotional and unforgettable moments too numerous to name, that one topped them all for me. Vin was seated at his position at the announcer table, leaned toward me with eyes wide and in a voice barely above a whisper, said just three words: 'Willie Mays. Wowww!' It was said with all the reverence of a young boy who had just seen his idol Mel Ott up close for the first time."

As Scully and his wife, Sandi, flew home Sunday afternoon, a line of firefighters were on the runway at Van Nuys Airport as the plane taxied to stop on the runway. The trucks then turned on their hoses and honored him the traditional retirement spray of water.

"I was already very emotional from that day," Scully said, "but to see that, I almost broke down again."

More Tributes As They Come

It's just been about three months since he said his last words on the air. In addition to an appearance on "Jimmy Kimmel Live," these things also happened:

Near the end of the Nov. 20 episode of the iconic Fox series "The Simpsons," a message filled the screen: "We'll Miss You, Vin Scully."

Executive producer and head writer Al Jean claimed responsibility, thanking Scully for all the years that, whenever a baseball broadcaster was included in an episode, Harry Shearer channeled his inner-Scully as the cartoon voice.

"Harry has done a terrific impression of Mr. Scully all these years and he has been very gracious about it and an inspiration to me and baseball fans everywhere," said Jean. "In our small way we wanted to honor his retirement."

Added Shearer: "He's one of the few exceptions of my general rule — that I only do characterizations of people of whom I have a critique. I grew up in L.A. with Vin Scully, he was with me when, as a child, I liked baseball, and he was all around me in the years since, when I couldn't have cared less about it.

"But regardless of my feelings about the game, my feeling about Scully remained the same throughout the years — a master broadcaster, a master storyteller. I've known a few of the guys at his level in various sports, and Scully was the gold standard in every way."

He received the Presidential Medal of Freedom Award from President Obama during a ceremony at the White House.

"It's not like I discovered penicillin," Scully said.

Vin Scully and baseball legend Willie Mays wave to fans during Scully's final broadcast, on Oct. 2, 2016 in San Francisco. (AP Images)

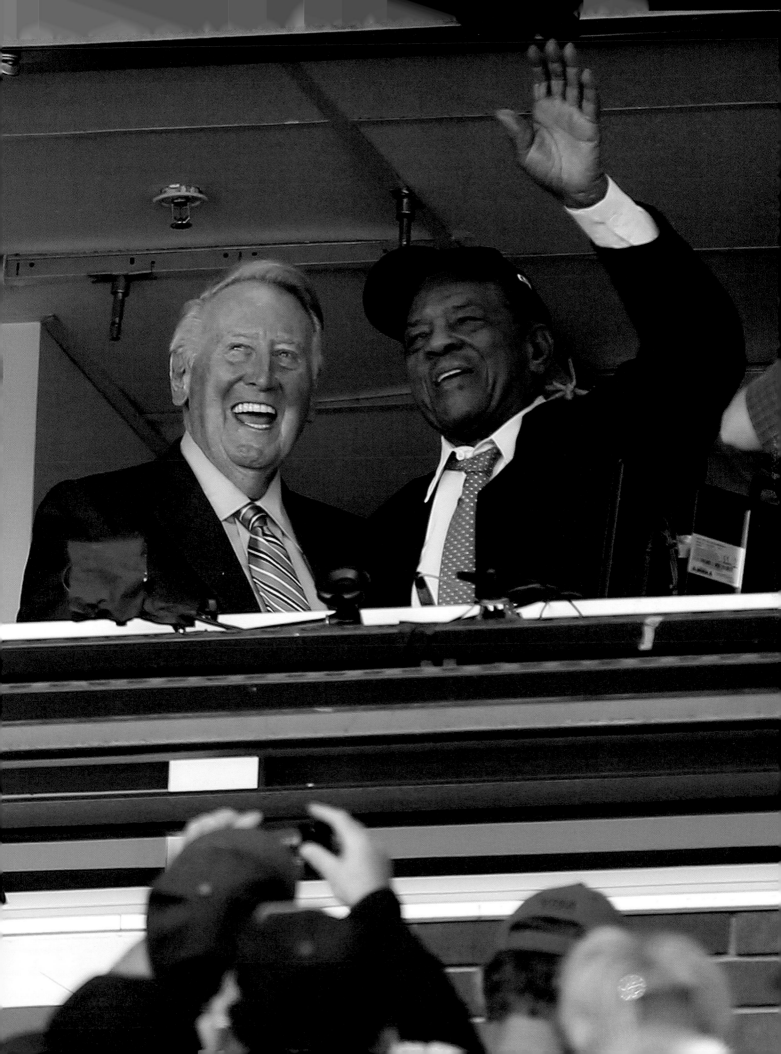

"When he heard about this honor, Vin asked with characteristic humility, 'Are you sure? I'm just an old baseball announcer,'" Obama remarked to the gathering. "And we had to inform him that, to Americans of all ages, you are an old friend."

While in Washington, D.C., Scully appeared on CBS' "Face the Nation," as host John Dickerson broke away from the usual politicans-in-the-news format to do a five-minute piece with him.

"Several people who work on the show are fans of his, with executive producer Mary Hager chief among them," said Dickerson. "But that wasn't enough of a reason to have him on. Scully is an American icon who has brought joy and excitement to millions. For all the reasons he was being celebrated at the White House, we wanted to talk to him.

"We've had a lot of politics this year. We wanted to do a show reflecting on the idea of gratitude for Thanksgiving. What drew us was his authenticity, his direct and sincere approach to his work and to life, and his humility. What a joy he was to talk to."

Scully, with the medal still around his neck, left Dickerson with a story that had the message: "Don't be afraid to dream."

Sports Illustrated included Scully in the finalists for its Sportsperson of the Year Award.

An SI cover piece on Scully in May included this from writer Tom Verducci: "Vin Scully is only the finest, most-listened-to baseball broadcaster that ever lived, and even that honorific does not approach proper justice to the man. He ranks with Walter Cronkite among America's most-trusted media personalities, with Frank Sinatra and James Earl Jones among its most-iconic voices, and with Mark Twain, Garrison Keillor and Ken Burns among its preeminent storytellers."

For the first time in its 19-year history, the Pasadena-based non-profit Baseball Reliquary included Scully as a candidate for its Shrine of the Eternals. It is a divine place known as the "People's Hall of Fame" to honor individuals "who have altered the baseball world in ways that supersede statistics."

Executive Director Terry Cannon explained that it was time.

"One of the many reasons was our appreciation for his generosity to the Baseball Reliquary and to the Shrine of the Eternals over the years," said Cannon. "Vin mentioned both the Reliquary and the Shrine on several occasions during his broadcasts in recent years … There has never been anyone of his stature in the world of baseball to acknowledge a grassroots, fan-based organization like the Reliquary, and that was certainly much appreciated by our members.

"Should Vin be elected, it would be my pleasure to let him know that he was now an Eternal himself. And, of course, I would not have to go into a long explanation as to what we are all about, which is often the case. Vin would know exactly what the significance is of induction."

The awards keep coming. Next month, the Southern California Sports Broadcasters will bestow its first Vin Scully Lifetime Achievement Award, and Scully would be the first recipient. The Dodgers will honor him again at the stadium on May 3 — adding him to their ring of retired player numbers.

We may be limited in finding new ways to notice and praise the goodness of Scully, but it's an easy call. We keep trying. Such is this eternally grateful recognition as well. ∎

The list of awards and achievements for Vin Scully is lengthy, but he'll be best remembered for his cherished connection with fans and unparalleled storytelling ability. (Los Angeles Daily News: Keith Birmingham)

SOUTHERN CALIFORNIA NEWS GROUP

Los Angeles Daily News
dailynews.com

THE ORANGE COUNTY REGISTER
ocregister.com

PRESS-TELEGRAM
presstelegram.com

DAILY BREEZE
dailybreeze.com

THE PRESS-ENTERPRISE
pe.com

Pasadena Star-News
pasadenastarnews.com

INLAND VALLEY DAILY BULLETIN
dailybulletin.com

THE SUN
sbsun.com

Redlands Daily Facts
redlandsdailyfacts.com

SAN GABRIEL VALLEY TRIBUNE
sgvtribune.com

Whittier Daily News
whittierdailynews.com

digital first
MEDIA

Local Brand Leaders — Known and Trusted for Over 100 Years

As premium local content providers, each of the SCNG newspapers has a long history of editorial excellence in their own respective markets — forming a special kind of trust and brand loyalty that readers really value. Exclusive local content sets the Southern California News Group apart, providing readers and users with news and information they won't find anywhere else. From local elections to their home team's top scores, when area residents need late-breaking news, SCNG newspapers, websites and mobile media are their number one resource.